DECEIVED
ON
PURPOSE

The New Age Implications
of the Purpose-Driven Church

Warren Smith

MOUNTAIN STREAM PRESS

Deceived on Purpose

©2004 Warren Smith
Second Edition: December 2004
Second Printing, January 2005
Third Printing, September 2005
Fourth Printing, November 2006
Fifth Printing, November 2007
Sixth Printing, January 2009

Mountain Stream Press
P.O. Box 1794
Magalia, CA 95954-1794

First Edition: August 2004, Conscience Press

Cover design by Vernon Rousseau.

To order additional copies of this book, call (800) 247-6553. For international orders, call (419) 281-1802.

Publisher's Cataloging-in-Publication Data

Smith, Warren, 1945-
    Deceived on purpose: the new age implications of the purpose-driven church / Warren Smith—2nd ed.
    1. Christianity 2. *The Purpose-Driven Life* / Rick Warren 3. The Purpose-Driven Church 4. New Age Spirituality

239   Library of Congress Control Number: 2004115014
ISBN 0-9763492-0-5
(previously published by Conscience Press, ISBN 0-9667071-3-3)

Printed in the United States of America.

Contents

Introduction

Rick Warren's Purpose-Driven Church campaign is being hailed by countless Christians everywhere as "a great move of God." With millions of Rick Warren's books already sold and thousands of churches involved in the movement, there has been real excitement about what is going on.

Nevertheless, a growing number of believers outside the movement have been uneasy about what is happening. Something doesn't seem quite right. Even with all of its apparent "success," the Purpose-Driven phenomenon is raising some red flags. Is it really a move of God? Is the Church in the midst of legitimate revival? Or is it all just "a little too good to be true?"

In 1984, my wife and I came out of the New Age movement. In my 1992 book, *The Light that was Dark*, I described our journey out of spiritual deception. We discovered that the spiritual teachings we had put our trust in were not from God and that the "Jesus" we had been following was not the real Jesus Christ. I wrote how we learned about the reality of a deceptive spirit world and how the Bible was filled with warnings about everything we had gotten so involved in. I explained how calculating and deceptive the spirit world had been in its dealings with us. I recounted the intensity of the spiritual warfare, as we saw through the deception and committed our lives to the true Jesus Christ. I warned Christian believers that the same false New Age "Christ" who had so deceived us was moving onto the world scene and was already in the process of deceiving the Church. I warned that Christians had to be very careful about the teachings they were accepting. In a more recent book, *Reinventing Jesus Christ: The New Gospel,* I reiterated and expanded upon these same warnings.

It was with this New Age background and perspective that I began my reading of *The Purpose-Driven Life* early in the fall of 2003. By then it had become a runaway national best seller. It seemed that almost everyone was being touched by Rick Warren in one way or another. Almost everything being said was very positive.

What I thought would be a pretty quick read turned out to be a lengthy process that included the writing of this book. Barely into my reading of *The Purpose-Driven Life,* I had immediate questions and concerns. And then, as I read a-long, one issue would seem to lead to another. It didn't take long to see that Rick Warren wasn't the only one who had definite purposes for the Purpose-Driven Church. It became very clear that our spiritual Adversary had his purposes, too. Because of my New Age background, I have written this book, *Deceived on Purpose,* to specifically address some of the New Age implications of these purposes.

This is an unorthodox and, at times, awkward book in that it attempts to recapture some of my process as I read through *The Purpose-Driven Life.* In a way, the chapters of this book are like a series of snapshots of what I was en-countering and what I was thinking as I read. Hopefully, what I went through will encourage you to take a closer look at some of the issues I raise concerning *The Purpose-Driven Life.*

Because I believe that Rick Warren is in the process of leading the Church astray, many people will regard this book as being "negative." But I don't look at it that way. Certain issues in *The Purpose-Driven Life* have been overlooked and need to be taken into account. The Apostle Paul said that "it is a shame" we have to talk about these kinds of things, but talk about them we must (Ephesians 5:12). The issues I raise are not personal issues between Rick Warren and myself.

Because Rick Warren's book is in the public domain and has been read by millions of people, I have chosen to respond to his book in this same public arena.

Because of my background, I have generally limited my discussion to what I believe are the New Age implications of *The Purpose-Driven Life*. This necessarily includes Rick Warren's relationship with Robert Schuller. I have made no attempt to "balance" my concerns with praise for Rick Warren because so many people have already done that. In fact, I would argue that my critique offers a "balance" to the largely predominant one-sided acclaim that he has mainly received up to this point. While this does not make for very uplifting reading, it keeps the focus on the specific issues that I felt needed to be addressed. Some of the evidence I present is strong. Some of it is rather circumstantial. But when all of the evidence is taken in its entirety, I believe there is a compelling case for believers to reconsider their involvement in the Purpose-Driven movement. Thanks for being open enough to read my concerns and, hopefully, to prayerfully consider what I have tried to convey.

—Warren Smith

A little leaven leaveneth the whole lump.
Galatians 5:9

Chapter 1

The Purpose-Driven Life

**Before you were born,
God planned *this moment* in your life.
It is no accident that you are holding this book.**[1]

Rick Warren
The Purpose-Driven Life, 2002

**[T]his book has arrived in your life
at the right and perfect time....
Everything happens in perfect order,
and the arrival of this book in your life
is no exception.**[2]

Neale Donald Walsch, New Age leader
Conversations with God: Book 2, 1997

Rick Warren's Purpose-Driven Church seemed to come at me from almost every conceivable direction late in the summer of 2003. I was working as a Hospice social worker on the California coast. Rick Warren's book *The Purpose-Driven Life* was riding high on the *New York Times* Best Sellers List. Friends of mine were in a Purpose-Driven Life study group. Hospice patients had *The Purpose-Driven Life* on their coffee tables. Purpose-Driven Church flyers were arriving in my mail box and showing up on community bulletin boards. Local churches were flying banners proclaiming they were "Purpose-Driven." It seemed that everywhere I turned there was Rick Warren and his Purpose-Driven Church.

When I finally sat down to read *The Purpose-Driven Life*,

I was aware that huge numbers of Christian leaders had endorsed the book. It seemed that most Christians were confident that God and Rick Warren were definitely up to something, and they wanted to be a part of it. Curiously, a friend of mine who was attending a Purpose-Driven Life study group was resisting the group. He said he preferred it when the group studied the Bible directly. He was reading *The Purpose-Driven Life* because other people in the group wanted to do it. But he was an apparent exception as most people seemed to be very excited about Rick Warren and his book.

New Age Update

The first time I encountered Rick Warren was in the spring of 2002, in a book entitled *From the Ashes: A Spiritual Response to the Attack on America*. The book was a collection of articles written by a wide variety of "spiritual leaders" and "extraordinary citizens" published in response to the events of September 11, 2001. Proceeds from the book were to go to the families of the 9/11 victims. I remember being intrigued by the fact that Christian leaders found themselves included in a book that also featured many familiar New Age leaders. Articles by Billy Graham, Bruce Wilkinson, Charles Colson, Max Lucado, Bill Hybels, Jerry Jenkins, Bishop T.D. Jakes and others were side by side with articles written by prominent New Age leaders like Neale Donald Walsch, the Dalai Lama and Starhawk the witch. I was not familiar with the man simply listed as "Pastor Rick Warren."

I discovered *From the Ashes* just after writing *Reinventing Jesus Christ: The New Gospel*. In my 2002 book, I had updated readers on significant recent New Age activity. I was concerned because Christian leaders were doing so little to warn believers about a New Age movement that had reinvented itself and was now referring to its teachings as the "new gospel" and the "New Spirituality." I found it particularly interesting that in *From the Ashes* Christian leaders not only found themselves in the company of top New Age leaders, they were now being directly challenged by some of these same New Age people.

New Age leader Neale Donald Walsch's article appeared just pages from Bishop T.D. Jakes' opening article. In his article, Walsch challenged religious leaders everywhere, including Rick Warren, Billy Graham, and every Christian leader in the book, in light of the events of September 11th to accept and preach the "new gospel" that "We are all one." After erroneously claiming that the Bible supports the idea that "We are all one," Walsch wrote:

> We must change ourselves. We must change the beliefs upon which our behaviors are based. We must create a different reality, build a new society....We must do so with new spiritual truths. We must preach a new gospel, its healing message summarized in two sentences:
>
> We are all one. *wrong!*
> Ours is not a better way, ours is merely another way.
>
> This 15-word message, delivered from every lectern and pulpit, from every rostrum and platform, could change everything overnight. I challenge every priest, every minister, every rabbi and religious cleric to preach this.[3]

I remember reading this and realizing how brazen the New Age was getting, and how deceptively appealing the idea of "Oneness" must sound to a terrified humanity still wondering when the next disaster might strike. What a clever way to present New Age teachings to a vulnerable world. But I was also thinking what a great opportunity it was for Christian leaders—particularly in this book—to contend for the faith by exposing the New Age teachings that were behind Walsch's seemingly "positive" exhortation. In Walsch's best-selling *Conversations with God* books, in which he purports to have actual "conversations with God," Walsch's "God" specifically defines what he means by the "new gospel" teaching that "We are all One." "God" tells Walsch:

God *is* creation.[4]

You are the Creator and the Created.[5] *oh oh!*

You are *already* a God. *You simply do not know it.*[6]

You are One with everyone and everything in the Universe—including God.[7]

There is only One of Us. You and I are One.[8]

If the Christian leaders in *From the Ashes* contended for the faith by responding to Walsch's New Age challenge, they could use the situation to delineate the significant differences between New Age teachings and the teachings of biblical Christianity. It was a unique opportunity for church leaders to expound upon the fact that God is *not* inherently "at One" with His creation and that man is *not* divine. They could explain that the Bible makes it very clear that humanity's only "Oneness" with God, and with each other, is through the person of Jesus Christ when we repent of our sins and choose to accept Him as our Lord and Savior.

> **For ye are all the children of God by faith in Christ Jesus**. For as many of you as have been baptized into Christ have put on Christ. There is neither Jew nor Greek, there is neither bond nor free, there is neither male nor female: **for ye are all one in Christ Jesus**.
> (Galatians 3:26-28; emphasis added)

Walsch's public challenge was a great opportunity for these Christian leaders to contend for the faith. But other than one lone pastor in Iowa,[9] I am not aware of anyone else publicly responding to Walsch's challenge.

Today, Walsch and other New Age leaders have accelerated their challenge to the Church by declaring that "God" has a 5-Step "PEACE Plan" to ultimately save the world through the establishment of a "New Spirituality." Part of this "New Spirituality" demands that Christians abandon their belief in Jesus Christ as their exclusive Lord and Savior. In a recent best-selling Walsch book, his New Age "God" has now openly declared, "The era of the Single Savior is over."[10]

But even with all of these open threats and challenges to biblical Christianity, most Christian leaders today continue to generally ignore almost anything having to do with New Age teachers and teachings. Over the last decade, as New Age teachings exploded in popularity, church leaders suddenly became very quiet about the New Age. Perhaps distracted by church growth concerns and tracking what they considered to be the latest "moves of God," church leaders seemed to be missing the latest moves of our spiritual Adversary. Excited about all of the "great" things they felt God was doing, they had become ignorant of what our Adversary was doing.

Hopefully a Berean Attitude

As I approached reading *The Purpose-Driven Life*, I hoped that Rick Warren would include "contending for the faith" as one of God's purposes for His people. It seemed obvious that if the Church was going to be at all effective it could not continue to pretend that the New Age wasn't happening. I wondered what Rick Warren might say, if anything, about the aggressive New Age challenge that was mounting against the Church.

I had a very definite process as I began reading, and reflecting, and following up on the things Rick Warren presented in his book. My intended attitude going into the reading was to approach his book with a Berean attitude. The Bible records in Acts 17:10-11 that the Apostle Paul commended the Bereans for comparing what he taught and said to Scripture. Rather than taking offense at what others might consider to be "criticism," Paul encouraged them to compare everything he was teaching to the Word of God. He did not regard those who sincerely measured what he said by Scripture as being "difficult," or "divisive," or having a "critical spirit." He understood that for truth to prevail in the Church, everyone's teachings—even his own—would have to be proven by the Word of God. He echoed this in I Thessalonians 5:21: "Prove all things; hold fast that which is good."

Meant to Be?

It is important for the reader to understand that when I was involved in the New Age movement I had been greatly misled by a number of seemingly "meant to be" types of experiences. I would later find out that many of these experiences had been cleverly orchestrated by a deceptive spirit world to make me think that what was happening in my life was coming from God—a seemingly chance encounter, a supernatural occurrence, something as simple as a book being innocently placed in my hands by a trusted friend. I had been told that "everything happens for a reason." "Nothing is by chance." "There are no accidents." "It's all part of God's plan." "It was *meant to be*."

A teaching from my former New Age text, *A Course in Miracles*, typifies this kind of "meant to be" thinking that is so prevalent in the New Age:

Remember that no one is where he is by accident, and chance plays no part in God's plan.[11]

I had been told by my New Age teachers that the Christian religion, with its "archaic" *King James Bible*, was not to be taken literally. And I had been deceptively led, by a series of cleverly devised "meant to be" type spiritual experiences, to believe that God was delivering "new revelation" to modern-day man. I had been supernaturally led to believe that *A Course in Miracles* was an extremely important part of this "new revelation," and that my involvement in it was "meant to be."

In *Reinventing Jesus Christ: The New Gospel,* I wrote:

We accepted the Course's interpretation of the Bible completely. It had a certain logic and seemed to make sense. We believed we were on the right path. Meaningful "coincidence" that had led us to the Course, and the supernatural signs that often accompanied our study appeared to confirm that we were where we were supposed to be.[12]

This idea that "there are no accidents" and that "everything happens for a reason" provided the spiritual justification for much of what I entered into in the New Age. If it was "meant to be" then I assumed that it *had* to be from God. It was "meant to be" because He loved me, and cared about me, and was reaching out to me in all of these life circumstances. He was leading me onwards and ever upwards on my spiritual journey. What other explanation could there be for all of these seemingly positive, spiritually uplifting, "synchronistic" events that were happening in my life?

But I had not read the Bible. I had no clue that I had a spiritual Adversary and that he was active in my life. I just followed the signs and kept moving along my seemingly destined spiritual path. I never questioned the origin of what was before me. I just assumed that everything was coming from God. In fact, almost all of my involvement in the New Age was initiated and sustained by a continuous series of these "meant to be" happenings. In my book *The Light That Was Dark*, I wrote:

> From that first psychic reading, I had been deceived. Led down a yellow brick road by pied piper spirits, I had, with the best intentions, landed in a metaphysical New Age where the Christ proclaimed was not the real Christ at all. A well-orchestrated and exquisitely timed series of supernatural synchronistic experiences had convinced me that my involvement in alternative spirituality was "meant to be." [13]

Testing the Spirits

As a believer, I came to understand that I could not just attribute everything that was happening in my life to God and "destiny." I realized that seemingly "meant to be" experiences can also be the deceptive work of our spiritual Adversary. I learned that everything has to be tested by Scripture and prayer. In the past, so many of my "meant to be" experiences had led me deeper and deeper into the teachings of the New Age. It was very humbling when I finally understood how spiritually deceived I had been. I learned the hard way that "meant to be" experiences don't always come from God.

So I was surprised, and obviously disappointed, that Rick Warren chose to begin his book by approaching the reader with the same device that I had so frequently encountered when I was in the New Age. On the dedication page in *The Purpose-Driven Life*, Rick Warren wrote:

This book is dedicated to you. Before you were born, God

planned *this moment* in your life. It is no accident that you
are holding this book.[14]

Certainly there is no argument that God arranges
specific circumstances and brings much good into our lives
through these events. But He also allows us to be con-
fronted by circumstances that test our faith. God doesn't
want us to just take Rick Warren's word, or anyone else's
word, about spiritual matters. We are not to just assume
things. God wants us to pray and to seek His wisdom in all
matters. He wants us to be like the Bereans and to measure
whatever we are being told by Scripture. It is just too easy
to get deceived—especially these days.

For Rick Warren to immediately tell his readers that his
book was a "meant to be" experience from God seemed
more than a little heavy-handed. Many New Age authors say
the same thing about their books. It can be very intimidat-
ing. When I was in the New Age I had been approached this
way many times. I thought that if I was being told this is
from God and that it's "meant to be" then I had better pay
attention and do what I was told. But I later learned through
harrowing spiritual experience that I could not just assume
things are from God because someone who seems to be
spiritually knowledgeable says so. Everything has to be
proven by the Word of God. Not everything is "destiny."
Not everything is "meant to be." There is a Deceiver.

Then, as I read down this same dedication page, I was
surprised to see that there was another apparent problem.
For some reason or another, Rick Warren was quoting
Eugene Peterson's *The Message* as if it were reliable and
authoritative Scripture. Not

Chapter 2

The Message and My 1994 Radio Warning

**Having a form of godliness,
but denying the power thereof:
from such turn away.**

2 Timothy 3:5

*I*first became aware of Eugene Peterson's "paraphrase" of the Bible in 1994 when I was doing a weekly segment on a syndicated radio show based on the East coast. The producer of the show entitled my weekly spot "Keeping Our Eye on the Enemy." It was based on a scripture from the First Book of Peter where he warned:

> Be sober, be vigilant; because your adversary the devil, as a roaring lion, walketh about, seeking whom he may devour. (1 Peter 5:8)

From my perspective of having been involved in New Age teachings, I would comment on best-selling New Age books and other issues that had New Age implications for the Church. On one program I expressed concern about author Eugene Peterson's new paraphrase of the Bible entitled *The Message*.

On the first page of *The Message*, the book is described as "a contemporary rendering of the Bible from the original languages, crafted to present its tone, rhythm, events, and ideas in everyday language." In other words, Peterson took the carefully translated words of the Holy Bible and put them into his own chosen words and idioms.

I expressed deep concern about *The Message* on my radio show. Anyone reading *The Message* should be able to quickly see how verses from Scripture often had their otherwise clear meanings obscured or even altered. Important details were sometimes omitted, while misleading words and phrases were often added. For example, when the disciples asked Jesus about His second coming and the end of the world, His reply in the Bible was very straightforward and clear:

> And Jesus answered and said unto them, Take heed that no man deceive you. For many shall come in my name, saying, I am Christ; and shall deceive many. (Matthew 24:4-5)

These important Bible verses had opened my eyes to truth back when I was involved in the New Age. *A Course in Miracles* and my other New Age teachings had taught me that love is all there is. Everything else is "fear" and "illusion." I had been told that because God is love, God is therefore *in* everyone and everything. There is *no separation* between God and His creation. Because everything is love and everything is "God," we are naturally "at One" with God and Christ and all creation. Lesson 124 in *A Course in Miracles* taught us to affirm, "Let me remember I am one with God."[1] When the "Jesus" of *A Course in Miracles* was asked if he was the Christ, he answered, "O yes, along with you."[2] According to *A Course in Miracles* and my other New Age teachings, all of humanity is divine. We are all "God" and we are all "Christ" and we are all "One." New Age

I remember the day when I read Matthew 24:4-5 and fully grasped what Jesus was saying. Thanks, in part, to that scripture I suddenly understood how deceived I had been. I wasn't Christ, or a part of Christ, at all. Jesus is the one and only Christ—there is *no* other. In my book *The Light that was Dark*, I described the importance of that scripture and its personal significance to me:

> Those of us who had believed the Course's Jesus—that he was the Christ and that we were too—were deceived...But in believing the Course and my other spiritual teachers, I had unwittingly become the very person that the real Jesus warned me to watch out for. "Take heed that no man deceive you. For many shall come in my name, saying, I am Christ; and shall deceive many."[3]

It was very sobering for me to realize that I was one of the people that Jesus was warning His followers to watch out for. This scripture enabled me to understand that my New Age belief that I was Christ was a definite false teaching. Because of that important scripture, I had been made to realize that Jesus' warning applied to the whole New Age movement that included my wife and me. This particular scripture helped to save my life. It gave me godly insight into the dynamics of the deception I had been a part of. But not so with Eugene Peterson's paraphrase of this same scripture. It fails to communicate what Jesus was *really* saying. When the disciples asked about Jesus' second coming and the end of the world, Peterson's paraphrase reads as follows:

> Jesus said, "Watch out for doomsday deceivers. Many leaders are going to show up with forged identities, claiming, 'I am Christ, the Messiah.' They will deceive a lot of people."[4]

By omitting the warning to let "*no man*" deceive you and paraphrasing it with only a general caution about "doomsday deceivers" and "leaders with forged identities," Peterson's paraphrase completely missed exposing all of us who were in the New Age believing we were Christ. It also allowed false Christs who portray themselves as "peace loving," and not as "doomsday deceivers," to slip under the scriptural radar. Jesus was not limiting His comments about false Christs to "doomsday deceivers." In fact, He wasn't specifying "doomsday deceivers" at all. His warning was all-encompassing. He said, "Take heed that no man deceive you." He was warning about *anyone* who says "I am Christ."

My wife and I were not "doomsday deceivers." We were not "leaders with forged identities." If we had been looking only at Eugene Peterson's paraphrase when we were un-believers, we would have never seen ourselves and the whole New Age movement in that prophetic passage of Scripture. But thanks to a *real* Bible, we were clearly shown that we were the subjects of Jesus' warning. Coming into the faith we had learned first-hand how the precision of a properly translated Bible can be the difference between truth and deception.

A verse in Hebrews beautifully conveys what we had learned and what I was trying to communicate to the radio audience about the difference between a poorly translated Bible and the true Word of God.

> For the word of God *is* quick, and powerful, and sharper than any two-edged sword, piercing even to the dividing asunder of soul and spirit, and of the joints and marrow, and *is* a discerner of the thoughts and intents of the heart. (Hebrews 4:12)

I was amazed that Peterson's book was being sold in Christian bookstores. I was concerned that if it ever became popular it could mislead a lot of people. I wondered how Peterson could just add, and subtract, and change God's Holy Word and not fear for his life. It seemed so obvious to me that part of the Bible's admonition to "work out your own salvation with fear and trembling" (Philippians 2:12) meant that we were not to "manhandle" the Word of God. In the Book of Revelation, God warns:

> For I testify unto every man that heareth the words of the prophecy of this book, If any man shall add unto these things, God shall add unto him the plagues that are written in this book: And if any man shall take away from the words of the book of this prophecy, God shall take away his part out of the book of life, and out of the holy city, and *from* the things which are written in this book. (Revelation 22:18-19)

However, when Peterson's book first came out there was no reason to think that it would one day be quoted *as the* Word of God. Back in 1994, *The Message* seemed to be just another strange sidelight in an already all too undiscerning Christian marketplace. No one that I was aware of was taking it seriously, much less referencing it, as authoritative Scripture. But now here it was again—Rick Warren was quoting from Peterson's paraphrase as if it were the Word of God.

Chapter 3

What Message?

Eugene Peterson's *The Message* seems to be very important to Rick Warren. It is the first Bible version that he quotes in *The Purpose-Driven Life*. He cites it at the bottom of his dedication page. He cites it again on the page that precedes his first chapter. He uses quotes from *The Message* to open and close his first chapter. Five of the six scriptures that Rick Warren cites in his first chapter all come from *The Message*. Even the title of the first chapter, "It All Starts with God," is taken from *The Message* paraphrase of Colossians 1:16, which appears right under the chapter heading.

> For everything, absolutely everything, above and below, visible and invisible,....everything got started in him and finds its purpose in him.[2]

The *King James Bible* translates Colossians 1:16 as follows:

> For by him were all things created, that are in heaven, and that are in earth, visible and invisible, whether *they be* thrones, or dominions, or principalities, or powers: all things were created by him, and for him.

It wasn't Peterson's use of the phrase "got started" instead of "created," or even the word "purpose" that jumped out at me, as much as his use of the phrase "above and below" instead of "heaven and earth." When I was in the New Age, it was well understood that the words "above and below" had metaphysical/New Age connotations and were routinely substituted for "heaven and earth." In fact, the term "as above, so below" was a commonly accepted New Age phrase.

In reading through *The Message*, I discovered that Peterson had actually inserted the entire phrase "as above, so below" into his paraphrase of the Lord's Prayer. I compared Peterson's version of the Lord's Prayer with the *King James* translation of that same prayer (Matthew 6:9-13). Peterson had deliberately substituted "as above, so below" in place of "in earth, as it is in heaven."

The Lord's Prayer: *The Message*

Our Father in heaven,
Reveal who you are.
Set the world right;
Do what's best—
as above, so below.
Keep us alive with three square meals.
Keep us forgiven with you and forgiving others.
Keep us safe from ourselves and the Devil.
You're in charge!
You can do anything you want!
You're ablaze in beauty!
Yes. Yes. Yes.[3] (Emphasis added)

In Colossians 1:16, Peterson again chose to use the terms "above" and "below" instead of the commonly accepted "heaven" and "earth" found in most Bible versions. The "above" and "below" in Colossians 1:16 is an obvious derivative form of the "as above, so below" he had used previously in his paraphrase of the Lord's Prayer. This derivative form of the more complete phrase "as above, so below" is also common to the New Age.

The fact that this whole "above" and "below" issue was presenting itself on the first page of the first chapter of Rick Warren's book was unsettling. Was I reading too much into this? Was there some other reasonable explanation for Eugene Peterson's use of the term "as above, so below" in the Lord's Prayer and its derivative form in Colossians 1:16? Or can there even be a good reason for inserting an occultic New Age term into the middle of the Lord's Prayer?

The Lord's Prayer: *King James Bible*

Our Father which art in heaven,
Hallowed be thy name.
Thy kingdom come.
Thy will be done
in earth, as *it is* **in heaven.**
Give us this day our daily bread.
And forgive us our debts, as we forgive our debtors.
And lead us not into temptation,
but deliver us from evil:
For thine is the kingdom,
and the power, and the glory, for ever.
Amen. (Emphasis added)

Ancient Egypt and Oneness

Right about the time I was looking into Eugene Peterson's use of the term "as above, so below," I was at a book sale at our local library. Almost lost amongst some cookbooks and business manuals was a book written and published by the editors of the *New Age Journal*. It was entitled *As Above, So Below*. I picked it up and began reading. In the introduction the chief editor of the book, Ronald S. Miller, had written:

> Thousands of years ago in ancient Egypt, the great master alchemist Hermes Trismegistus, believed to be a contemporary of the Hebrew prophet Abraham, proclaimed this fundamental truth about the universe: "As above, so below; as below, so above." This maxim implies that the transcendent God beyond the physical universe and the immanent God within ourselves are one. Heaven and Earth, spirit and matter, the invisible and the visible worlds form a unity to which we are intimately linked.[4]

He continued his explanation by quoting Sufi scholar Reshad Field.

> "As above, so below" means that the two worlds are instantaneously seen to be one when we realize our essential unity with God....The One and the many, time and eternity, are all One."[5] (Ellipsis dots in original)

The *New Age Journal* editor went on to state that old forms of religion no longer serve people, and that the term "as above, so below" describes the "emerging spirituality" that is quickly moving onto the world's scene. He concluded his introduction to *As Above, So Below* by writing:

> The breadth of this exploration suggests that we are living in an age of spiritual reinvention, a transitional age that

leaves the safety and security of the known to seek out the new, the untested, the possible.[6]

Moving from the library book sale to the Internet, I put "as above, so below" into the Google search engine to see what would come up. There were countless references. The very first reference listed by Google for "as above, so below" read:

> This phrase comes from the beginning of The Emerald Tablet and embraces the entire system of traditional and modern magic which was inscribed upon the tablet in cryptic wording by Hermes Trismegistus. The significance of this phrase is that it is believed to hold the key to all mysteries. All systems of magic are claimed to function by this formula. "That which is above is the same as that which is below'... The universe is the same as God, God is the same as man...."[7]

As I checked out the most popular websites for "as above, so below," each one described the term as having the same occultic, mystical, eastern, New Age, esoteric, and magical sources. One site stated:

> This ancient phrase, "As above, so below" describes the Oneness of All That Is.[8]

The phrase "AS ABOVE, SO BELOW" headlined a page from a Theosophical website containing "esoteric" teachings espoused by New Age matriarch Alice A. Bailey. A derivative form of the term—similar to Peterson's abbreviated use of "above and below" in Colossians 1:16—appeared on the website in a quote from Theosophy founder Helena Blavatsky's pioneering New Age work, *The Secret Doctrine*:

> Above, the Son is the whole KOSMOS;
> below, he is MANKIND.[9]

To see if there was any other explanation for Peterson's use of this mystical New Age phrase, I put the term *as above, so below* along with the term *Christianity* into the search engine of the computer I was using. There were only seven immediate references. None of them had anything to do with biblical Christianity. The first reference was entitled "Mystical Christianity" and said:

> ...to help the seeker of an inner spiritual path find resources to aid their spiritual journey towards a mystical and magickal Christianity.[10]

In all of my searching, I could find no good reason for Peterson using "as above, so below" in his paraphrase of the Lord's Prayer. Nor could I find any good reason for his use of the obvious "above and below" derivative in his Colossians 1:16 paraphrase, which Rick Warren used at the very beginning of his book to initiate his readers into *The Purpose-Driven Life*.

So What?

I guess if Rick Warren or anyone else says, "So what?" I would say, "So how come?" How come Eugene Peterson inserted a universally accepted, mystical New Age term right into the middle of the Lord's Prayer? And why does a derivative of the saying show up in his paraphrase of Colossians 1:16? Even if you thought there was some "good" reason for using the term "as above, so below," why would you? Why would you choose a term that so clearly has its origins in the magic of ancient Egypt and is so heavily identified today with the New Age and the New Spirituality?

"As above, so below" agrees with the "immanent" New Age view that God is not only outside of creation, but also *within* creation. It means that God is "in" everyone and everything. It perfectly denotes the New Age concept of "Oneness" and provides apparent support for the New Age contention that "We are all One."

Seeker Friendly?

I tried to imagine what it would be like for a confused New Ager today coming into a Purpose-Driven Church that uses *The Message*, and finding this popular New Age phrase right in the middle of the Lord's Prayer. Or what it would be like for that person to be handed a copy of Rick Warren's book, only to find an abbreviated form of this same New Age phrase as part of the lead-off scripture introducing them to *The Purpose-Driven Life*. This hardly seemed to be the way to introduce the Gospel of Jesus Christ to an unbelieving New Ager.

Rick Warren's reintroduction of *The Message* into my life only reinforced the concerns I had originally voiced on the radio when Peterson's book first came out. Why was Rick Warren so drawn to *The Message*? *The Message* not only obscured prophetic scriptures like Matthew 24:3-5, it also introduced paraphrased material like "as above, so below," which made it appear that some of the teachings of the Bible were "at One" with the teachings of the New Age.

In *Reinventing Jesus Christ: The New Gospel*, I had observed:

> And it is, indeed, very disturbing to see many Christian leaders today using many of the same words and expressions commonly used by their [New Age] "new gospel" counterparts.[11]

> Unfortunately, undiscerning Christian leaders have not adequately exposed these [New Age] "new gospel" teachings and, as a result, the spirit behind the "new gospel" has entered the Church.[12]

Chapter 4

The Kindly Christian Widow

Heaven and earth shall pass away,
but my words shall not pass away.

Matthew 24:35

When I was in the New Age and very involved with *A Course in Miracles*, I was working for a Northern California agency as a program coordinator serving the developmentally disabled. One day while I was visiting the elderly widowed mother of one of my clients the subject of religion came up. After asking me what I believed, she listened politely as I shared my enthusiasm for the New Age teachings of *A Course in Miracles*. As I described what I believed, she smiled sweetly but didn't say much. When I finished talking, she excused herself for a moment and went into another room. When she returned she was holding a large, blue *King James Bible*. She wanted me to have it. Not wanting to offend her, and noting its color was a perfect match with my Course in Miracles books, I accepted her gift.

Several years later, as my wife and I were beginning to understand how deceived we had been by *A Course in Miracles* and our other New Age teachings, it was this kind woman's *King James Bible* that we continually turned to for support and counsel. It sharply contrasted the differences between the New Age "gospel" and the Gospel of Jesus Christ and was instrumental in our ultimate conversion to the Christian faith. And we have continued to use the *King*

James Bible for the last twenty years. It has been our guide in everything we do. We thought it was beautifully written, and we found it to be very readable. Occasional outdated words are often defined by their context or can be easily looked up in a matter of seconds. More than anything, though, the teachings and doctrine of the *King James Bible* have always rung true.

Bible versions only became an issue for us when my book *The Light that was Dark* was in the process of being published by Moody Press. Moody insisted on converting many of my *King James* quotes into a newer version. They said they had to make my book more "readable" and "seeker friendly," so I reluctantly went along with their request. I would not do that today.

I have never understood why church leaders have felt it necessary to downplay and almost apologize for the *King James* translation. As "seekers," the *King James Bible* had met us *right where* we were at. It might not have been "spiritually correct" for that kind woman to give an unbeliever a *King James Bible* instead of a newer version, but I will be forever grateful that she did. It helped to save our lives.

No Legitimate Reason?

Having only used one Bible all these years, I wanted to understand why Rick Warren felt the need to use fifteen different Bible versions and paraphrases in *The Purpose-Driven Life.* In the back of his book I found this explanation:

> This book contains nearly a thousand quotations from Scripture. I have intentionally varied the Bible translations used for two important reasons. First, no matter how wonderful a translation is, it has limitations....
>
> Second, and even more important, is the fact that we often miss the full impact of familiar Bible verses, *not* because of

poor translating, but simply because they have become so familiar!....Therefore I have deliberately used paraphrases in order to help you see God's truth in new, *fresh* ways. English-speaking people should thank God that we have so many different versions to use for devotional reading.[1]

I couldn't really relate to what Rick Warren was saying about "limitations" and overly "familiar" verses. I had always had full confidence in the *King James* translation, and familiar verses became more and more precious as their truth continued to resound in our lives year after year. Of the fifteen different versions he used, *The Message* was clearly Rick Warren's favorite. In *The Purpose-Driven Life* he rarely referred to the *King James Bible.* I found his strange reason *why* in his 1995 book *The Purpose-Driven Church:*

Read Scripture from a newer translation. With all the wonderful translations and paraphrases available today, there is no legitimate reason for complicating the Good News with four-hundred-year-old English. Using the King James Version creates an unnecessary cultural barrier.... Clarity is more important than poetry.[2]

No "legitimate reason" to read the *King James Bible?* I remember reading that and being amazed. How could he possibly teach something that was so untrue? The *King James Bible* had not "complicated" the "Good News" for my wife and I when we were lost in the New Age—it *had* provided much needed clarity by exposing the deceptiveness of our New Age teachings. In *The Light that was Dark* I commented:

When we could finally see through the spiritual deception, most of the Scriptures that we had been reading clicked into place. It was as if scales had fallen from our eyes, and suddenly the New Testament was flooded with light. Though we had a lot to learn about other aspects of the faith, it was apparent that we were, by virtue of our having been so thoroughly deceived, already well-versed in the Bible's description of deception.[3]

> Sometimes we thought we were confusing everyone but ourselves. Disappointed but not disheartened by our friends, and discouraged but not disillusioned by some of the churches, we were nevertheless determined to tell our story of the reality of evil and of the power and majesty of the real Christ—how it was the Bible, not our alternative spiritual teachings, that read clearer and truer than the morning paper.[4]

God had used the *King James Bible* in a mighty way to reveal the truth. It had pulled us out of the New Age and put us on solid ground. Its straightforward warnings and teachings were clear and true. If we had been dependent on *The Message*, or some of the other Bible versions that Rick Warren uses, we might still be in the New Age today. It was the clarity and precision of our *King James Bible* that had exposed the deception behind our New Age teachings. And it is the clarity and precision of our *King James Bible* that continues to expose these same New Age teachings that are creeping into the Church today. I just thank God no one put something like *The Message* in my hands when I was in the New Age. And I thank God for kindly Christian widows.

Chapter 5

Enter Robert Schuller

**Our very survival "as a species depends on hope.
And without hope we will lose the faith
that we can cope."**[1]

Robert Schuller (quoting author Rene Dubos)
Self-Esteem: The New Reformation, 1982

**Hope is as essential to your life as air and water.
You need hope to cope."**[2]

Rick Warren
The Purpose-Driven Life, 2002

I knew I was being spiritually led when I was in the New Age. I just didn't know that I was being led by a deceptive spirit world. I didn't even know that there was a deceptive spirit world or that there were such things as deceptive spirits. I didn't realize that deceptive spirits could present themselves as "God" and "Jesus" and the "Holy Spirit." I didn't know that the Bible warns about these deceptive spirits and tells us to test the spirits to make sure that we are not being deceived by "another Jesus," "another spirit," and "another gospel" (1 John 4:1; 2 Corinthians 11:3-4).

Years ago, as previously mentioned, I had a number of seemingly "meant to be" supernatural experiences that made me believe my New Age teachings were from God and I was on the right path. I had no idea there was a Deceiver and that I was being spiritually deceived. It all started with what seemed to be an innocent psychic reading. Trying to please a woman I had just met, I agreed to see a friend of a friend of hers who was a traveling psychic from Canada. Somewhat skeptical going into the reading, I was amazed at how much the psychic seemed to know about me. Over the course of the reading, she was describing things that I had never shared with anyone. This gave her credibility in my eyes and set me up for what happened later in our session. In *The Light that was Dark*, I described what happened:

> It was toward the end of the reading that I first noticed the whirling sensation over my head. I tried to ignore it, but it wouldn't go away. It was a strange but not unpleasant feeling that seemed to flutter and vibrate and even tingle above me. I was startled when Bonnie picked up on it.
>
> "Are you aware that there is a ball of light over your head?"
>
> I was dumbfounded. A ball of light? Is *that* what I was feeling? This was getting a little wild.
>
> I told Bonnie that I had been feeling *something* over my head but didn't know what it was. She said it again.
>
> "It's a ball of light."
>
> For a moment I tried to understand what a ball of light was doing over my head. Then I asked the obvious.
>
> "Why is there a ball of light over my head?"
>
> "You are being shown that you have a lot of help on the other side," she said matter-of-factly.
>
> "What do you mean by 'the other side'?"
>
> "The spirit world," was her quick reply. "Family and loved ones who have passed away, as well as angels and other spirits who for whatever reasons are sympathetic to your life. They are making themselves known to you. They are reaching out to you and letting you know that they are available if you want their help." Bonnie was smiling; she seemed pleased by this show of support.
>
> I was intrigued that there was a spirit world and flattered

by its interest in me. I asked Bonnie to elaborate.

"Those on the other side know what you are going through. Although they are making themselves known to you, they will not involve themselves in your life without your permission. If you want their help you will have to ask."....

I sat back in my chair trying to comprehend it. *How amazing, I thought, that we can reach out to the spirit world. A spiritual dimension is really out there, willing and able to help us.* I knew in that moment that I wanted its help. I understood that the ball of light had come at a perfect time—in the reading and in my life. It had given me a much needed sense of validation. I felt better about myself knowing that somewhere out there in the universe I was really cared for. Suddenly I didn't feel alone. As far as I was concerned, the ball of light had been an act of compassion, and I was grateful.[3]

I went on to describe in my book how later that same day I prayed and asked all those on "the other side" to come into my life. Shortly after that, my life took off like a rocket ship into the New Age, as what I thought were "meant to be" experiences from God started streaming into my life. I did not understand that I had just unwittingly involved myself with a deceptive spirit world that is fully described and warned about in the Bible. It wasn't until five years later that I came to understand what happens when you involve yourself with spiritual leadings that are not from God but from His spiritual Adversary. Many New Age leaders today describe similar supernatural experiences that initiated, or further reinforced, their involvement in the deceptive teachings of the New Age.

Gerald Jampolsky

In his book *Teach Only Love*, psychiatrist Gerald Jampolsky described how he "had one of the strangest and most amazing experiences" in his life after being brushed with a peacock feather and touched by the Indian guru Swami Baba Muktananda. Jampolsky described the effects of the experience at length and how the guru's touch had resulted in a "radical shift" in his "belief system."[4]

> After sitting quietly for five minutes, my body began to quiver and shake in an indescribable manner. Beautiful colors appeared all around me, and it seemed as though I had stepped out of my body and was looking down at it. Part of me wondered if someone had slipped me a hallucinogenic drug or if I was going crazy.
>
> I saw colors whose depth and brilliance were beyond anything I had ever imagined. I began to talk in tongues—a phenomenon I had heard about but discredited. A beautiful beam of light came into the room and I decided at that moment to stop evaluating what was happening and simply be one with the experience, to join it completely.[5]
>
> Although I usually have a high energy level, for the next three months it was heightened and I required very little sleep. I was filled with an awareness of love unlike anything I had known before. The power of this experience made me want to take a new look at everything I was calling real, because I had glimpsed a reality that is not limited to the physical plane. This was an important step toward a complete reappraisal of my concepts about God and spirituality. Although I didn't know it at the time, this experience was to prepare me for my encounter with *A Course in Miracles* a year or so later. But in the meantime, I was still struggling.[6]

That next year, 1975, Jampolsky's good friend Judith Skutch, who was soon to become the publisher of *A Course in Miracles*, gave him a copy of the Course while it was still in manuscript form.[7] In *Journey Without Distance: The Story Behind A Course In Miracles*, author Robert Skutch wrote:

Jerry was one of the first recipients of the Xeroxed manuscript. It came to him at a particularly appropriate time, for he had recently gone through a painful divorce and was drinking heavily. He had begun to question his purpose in life...[8]

In his book *Love Is Letting Go of Fear*, Jampolsky describes how one day while reading the Course, he heard an "inner voice" telling him, "Physician, heal thyself: this is your way home."[9] Supernaturally impressed by the inner voice and by what he was reading, Jampolsky became an almost immediate convert to the "God" and "Christ" of *A Course in Miracles*. He has been a prominent *A Course in Miracles* proponent and New Age leader ever since. In 1979, his best-selling book about *A Course in Miracles* entitled *Love Is Letting Go of Fear* was published. It was this Jampolsky book that led me to *A Course in Miracles* and prompted me to go even more deeply into the teachings of the New Age.

Marianne Williamson

New Age leader Marianne Williamson claims that a number of years ago, after a "nervous breakdown" and in the midst of her study of *A Course in Miracles*, she met "Jesus." One night she said she felt the presence of "Jesus" by her bed. "I was not normal and I knew it," she said. Not understanding the deceptive spirit world and the importance of testing the spirits, she started talking to the presence that she assumed was the real Jesus:

"So I said to Jesus, 'Look, if you can give me back my life, if you can restore me somehow, then I will do whatever you want me to do for the rest of my life.' Like people make a pact with the devil, I made a pact with Jesus."[10]

Williamson's career skyrocketed after her book *A Return*

to *Love: Reflections on the Principles of A Course in Miracles* was enthusiastically endorsed by Oprah Winfrey on *The Oprah Winfrey Show*. Williamson has been an internationally recognized New Age/new gospel leader ever since. She and Neale Donald Walsch co-founded The Global Renaissance Alliance—which includes many prominent New Age/new gospel leaders—to further the New Age teachings that would soon be alternately described as the "New Spirituality." The "Jesus" that Williamson follows is the false New Age "Jesus" of *A Course in Miracles*, not the real Jesus of the Bible.

Neale Donald Walsch

New Age/new gospel leader Neale Donald Walsch was a disillusioned and depressed former radio talk show host, public relations professional, and longtime metaphysical seeker[11] when he sat down one night and wrote God an angry letter.[12] He was shocked when "God" seemed to answer his letter by speaking directly to him through an inner voice. That evening, and in future "conversations," Walsch transcribed all of the dictated answers to his questions. These conversations were published in 1995 as Walsch's *Conversations with God: Book 1*. The book was the first in a series of best-selling *Conversations with God* books. He is one of the most visible and outspoken New Age leaders today as he directly challenges everyone to accept the "new gospel" of the "New Spirituality" that "We are all One."

With supernatural experiences seeming to validate so many of us at critical times in our lives, most of us did not doubt the seeming "truth" of our experiences. But we didn't know about the Bible's warning to "try" the spirits (1 John 4:1) to make sure they weren't deceptive spirits delivering false teachings. Many other New Age leaders, and countless numbers of day to day people like myself, were propelled into the New Age by similar encounters with the spirit world.

Bernie Siegel

In June of 1978, a Connecticut physician named Bernie Siegel attended a workshop that would completely change his life, including the way he practiced medicine. As a result of a spiritual experience in this workshop—a guided visualization—he would eventually become a best-selling author and New Age leader. In his book *Love, Medicine & Miracles*, he described this guided visualization:

> In June 1978, my practice of medicine changed as a result of an unexpected experience I had at a teaching seminar Oncologist O. Carl Simonton and psychologist Stephanie Matthews (then his wife) gave a workshop—Psychological Factors, Stress, and Cancer—at the Elmcrest Institute in Portland, Connecticut.[13]

> The Simontons taught us how to meditate. At one point they led us in a directed meditation to find and meet an inner guide. I approached this exercise with all the skepticism one expects from a mechanistic doctor. Still, I sat down, closed my eyes, and followed directions. I didn't believe it would work, but if it did I expected to see Jesus or Moses. Who else would dare appear inside a surgeon's head?

> Instead I met George, a bearded, long-haired young man wearing an immaculate flowing white gown and a skullcap. It was an incredible awakening for me, because I hadn't expected anything to happen....

> George was spontaneous, aware of my feelings, and an excellent adviser. He gave me honest answers, some of which I didn't like at first....

> All I know is that he has been my invaluable companion

ever since his first appearance. My life is much easier now, because he does the hard work.[14]

Since that initial spiritual encounter, Siegel has become a leading New Age author and spokesperson. Providing "hope" by fusing modern day medicine with New Age teachings and practices, Siegel has introduced New Age concepts into the professional medical community and to cancer patients everywhere. In *Friendship with God*, Neale Donald Walsch wrote that Bernie Siegel was the "first celebrity endorsement" he received for his first book, *Conversations with God: Book 1*. Walsch said that "it helped book buyers, who might have been skittish about a previously unpublished author, see the value of what I had produced."[15]

Today, Siegel continues to influence countless numbers of people in his role as a New Age leader. In his books and workshops he encourages people to do guided meditations and visualizations—just as he once did—to initiate contact with their own personal spirit guides. Siegel openly endorses the teachings of *A Course in Miracles* and currently serves on the Board of Advisors of Jerry Jampolsky's *A Course in Miracles*-based Attitudinal Healing Center in Northern California.[16]

Why Siegel?

I describe Bernie Siegel at length because I was about to discover that Rick Warren suddenly and inexplicably made reference to Bernie Siegel in Chapter Three of *The Purpose-Driven Life*. He used Siegel's name in conjunction with remarks he was making about people who have "hope" and a "deep sense of life purpose." The reference followed Rick Warren's strange characterization of Isaiah and Job as two men who exemplified life "without purpose" and life "without God."

The reader is given no explanation as to who Bernie Siegel is and, therefore, has no idea that Rick Warren was using the remark of a New Age leader to reference the importance of having "hope" and "purpose" in their life. Particularly for someone like myself who came out of the New Age, it was extremely bizarre to see Rick Warren's remarks linking hope with the New Age leader Bernie Siegel rather than with Isaiah and Job. His skewed comments were very misleading. Rick Warren wrote:

> Without God, life has no purpose, and without purpose, life has no meaning. Without meaning, life has no significance or hope. In the Bible, many different people expressed this hopelessness. Isaiah complained, "*I have labored to no purpose; I have spent my strength in vain and for nothing.*" Job said, "*My life drags by—day after hopeless day*" and "*I give up; I am tired of living. Leave me alone. My life makes no sense.*" The greatest tragedy is not death, but life without purpose.
>
> Hope is as essential to your life as air and water. You need hope to cope. Dr. Bernie Siegel found he could predict which of his cancer patients would go into remission by asking, "Do you want to live to be one hundred?" Those with a deep sense of life purpose answered yes and were the ones most likely to survive. Hope comes from having a purpose.[17]

Isaiah and Job Without Purpose?

After quoting the situational complaints of Isaiah and Job, Rick Warren stated, as quoted above, "The greatest tragedy is not death, but life without purpose." In reality, Isaiah's "complaining" had nothing to do with "a life without purpose" or being "without God." Rather, it had to do with the fact that Isaiah was finding the prophetic role that God had assigned to him to be very discouraging. He was trying to warn the people that their religious leaders were leading them astray.

> O my people, they which lead thee cause thee to err, and destroy the way of thy paths. (Isaiah 3:12)

Isaiah was trying to tell the people they were being deceived, but it seemed that no one was listening. Isaiah was *not* "without purpose." He was just deeply frustrated with Israel's leaders and the people who were blindly following them.

Using the *New International Version*, Rick Warren chose to quote only half of Isaiah 49:4 in trying to make his case that Isaiah was a man "without purpose" and "without God."

> "I have labored to no purpose; I have spent my strength in vain and for nothing." [18]

The whole NIV verse paints a completely different picture.

> But I said, "I have labored to no purpose; I have spent my strength in vain and for nothing. *Yet what is due me is in the Lord's hand, and my reward is with my God.*" [19]
> (Emphasis added)

The *King James Bible* makes Isaiah's sense of purpose and faith in God even clearer in this same passage.

> Then I said, I have laboured in vain, I have spent my strength for nought, and in vain: *yet surely my judgement is with the Lord, and my work with my God.* (Emphasis added)

Matthew Henry, a respected Bible commentator, wrote this about Isaiah's "complaint" in Isaiah 49:4:

> He comforts himself under this discouragement with this consideration, that it was the cause of God in which he was engaged and the call of God that engaged him in it: *Yet surely my judgement is with the Lord*, who is the Judge of all, *and my work with my God*, whose servant I am. His comfort is, and it may be the comfort of all faithful ministers, when they see little success of their labours...That, however it be, it is a righteous cause that they are pleading. They are with God, and for God; they are on his side, and workers together with him....The unbelief of men gives them no cause to suspect the truth of their doctrine...[20]

Matthew Henry rightly points out that Isaiah was anything but purposeless. He may have been discouraged that no one seemed to be listening to him, but he never lost his sense of purpose or his faith in God. The same is true of God's servant Job, whose despair and temporary discouragement in the midst of great loss had nothing to do with his overall commitment and devotion to God.

The Hope and Purpose of Robert Schuller

Rick Warren could have wonderfully introduced hope and purpose through the godly lives of Isaiah and Job. Yet he chose to use them as examples of men who were without hope, purpose or God in their lives. Instead, he used a New Age leader to preface his remarks about having a true hope that comes from having a "deep sense of purpose." Looking again at what he wrote:

> Hope is as essential to your life as air and water. You need hope to cope. Dr. Bernie Siegel found he could predict which of his cancer patients would go into remission by asking, "Do you want to live to be one hundred?" Those with a deep sense of life purpose answered yes and were the ones most likely to survive. Hope comes from having a purpose.[21]

As I read this whole section in *The Purpose-Driven Life*, I kept asking myself: why would Rick Warren want to introduce his readers, even indirectly, to a New Age leader like Bernie Siegel? Why would he preface his whole discussion about the importance of having "hope" and a "deep sense of life purpose" by referring to a man whose own hope and purpose are so totally invested in the false teachings of the New Age? A believer's *true hope* is not based on perceptions of longevity or the false hopes of this world. It is based *only* in the person of Jesus Christ. *He* is our hope (I Timothy 1:1).

What helped to finally clarify the matter for me was my discovery that much of Rick Warren's seemingly spontaneous discussion about hope and purpose—even his reference to Bernie Siegel—could be found in the writings and teachings of Robert Schuller.

I became aware of Schuller's influence while searching the Internet in an attempt to understand why Rick Warren might be citing Bernie Siegel in reference to "hope." I discovered an *Hour of Power* sermon in which Robert Schuller referenced Bernie Siegel in regards to this same issue of "hope." After describing Bernie Siegel as "one of the greatest doctors of the 20th Century," Schuller stated:

> Dr. Siegel said that he's been accused of building false hope and he likes to tell people that the only false hope is giving them no hope.[22]

I was not that surprised that Robert Schuller would use a New Age leader to make a sermon point about hope. But why would Rick Warren? Bernie Siegel's New Age hope *is* a false hope—and no hope at all. Was it Schuller's obvious high regard for Bernie Siegel, and Rick Warren's high regard for Robert Schuller, that prompted Rick Warren to make this reference to Siegel in *The Purpose-Driven Life*?

Hoping and Coping Back in 1982

My sense that Rick Warren and Robert Schuller's references to Bernie Siegel were more than coincidence was later confirmed when I was researching some of Robert Schuller's previous writings and reading through his 1982 book *Self-Esteem: The New Reformation*. As I read along in this book, I suddenly stumbled upon some Schuller material regarding "hope and purpose" that sounded just like Rick Warren. Schuller was citing sociobiologist Rene Dubos' book *Celebration of Life* as the source of his remarks.

In his 1982 book *Self-Esteem: The New Reformation*, Schuller wrote:

> Our very survival "as a species depends on hope. And without hope we will lose the faith that we can cope."[23]

Twenty years later, in his 2002 book *The Purpose-Driven Life*, Rick Warren making no reference to Schuller or Dubos wrote:

> Hope is as essential to your life as air and water. You need hope to cope.[24]

It seemed that in *The Purpose-Driven Life*, Rick Warren had combined the Schuller reference to Bernie Siegel with other material that Schuller had written back in 1982. He even turned the words "hope" and "cope" into a "hope to cope" rhyme worthy of the man he was so obviously emulating.

But the use of Schuller material didn't stop there. Right after the unattributed "hope to cope" reference, Rick Warren introduced "hope" and "purpose" to his millions of readers by citing Jeremiah 29:11—one of Robert Schuller's signature scriptures. Rick Warren wrote:

If you have felt hopeless, hold on! Wonderful changes are going to happen in your life as you begin to live it on purpose. God says, *"I know what I am planning for you.... 'I have good plans for you, not plans to hurt you. I will give you hope and a good future.'"* [25]

Sixteen years before Rick Warren's *The Purpose-Driven Life*, Robert Schuller had also introduced "hope" and "purpose" by citing Jeremiah 29:11. In his 1986 book *Be Happy You are Loved*, Schuller had written:

"For I know the plans I have for you, says the Lord. They are plans for good and not for evil, to give you a future and a hope." (Jer. 29:11 TLB)

This Bible verse says plainly that God has a plan and a dream and it includes you. You were born for a purpose. [26]

Apparently, Robert Schuller had been talking about "purpose" for years. In *Self-Esteem: The New Reformation*, Schuller had introduced "purpose" in relation to what he described as "God's dream" for our life.

God chooses us to serve his purpose. "You did not choose me, but I chose you." Our self-esteem is rooted in our divine call. God's dream for our life and work gives purpose and pride to our life....

God's plan and purpose calls for us to succeed and not to fail. [27]

In his first televised sermon to Russia on December 25, 1989, Schuller began his telecast by citing Jeremiah 29:11 to preface his remarks about having hope and purpose. He concluded his sermon by referring back to Jeremiah 29:11 and using that specific scripture as a call for peace between the two countries. [28] Schuller described the importance of Jeremiah 29:11 in his own life in the introduction to his

1977 book, *Daily Power Thoughts.*

> In preparing this book, my dream is to help you enjoy the beautiful possibilities God has available for you.
>
> A very important scripture in my life is Jeremiah 29:11...[29]

New Age Praise for Robert Schuller

But Rick Warren was not the only one who seemed to be impressed with the writings and teachings of Robert Schuller. I was soon to find out that Bernie Siegel had personally endorsed Robert Schuller's 1995 book, *Prayer: My Soul's Adventure With God.* This endorsement appeared on the opening page of Schuller's book:

> This is a beautiful book of value to all people....Robert Schuller's newest book reaches beyond religion and information to what we all need—spirituality, inspiration, and understanding. Read it and live a life with meaning.[30]

Later, as I was forced to read more of Schuller's books—because of his obvious spiritual influence on Rick Warren—I found that Schuller had recommended guided meditations and visualizations,[31] not unlike the kind that linked Bernie Siegel up with his spirit guide George. It was no wonder that Schuller and Siegel expressed mutual affection for one another's work.

Robert Schuller actually described an incident that reminded me of Bernie Siegel's encounter with his spirit guide George. Ill-advisedly using relaxation and meditation techniques before praying to God concerning an eating problem he had, Schuller claimed to have had an encounter with "Jesus." Schuller wrote:

> I knew that I was hopelessly addicted so I went into a time

of relaxation, meditation, and two-way prayer.

> In a matter of seconds I can get myself in such a state of relaxation where I am not at all conscious of my body weight, but sense that I am floating suspended in space. And this is when I go into two-way prayer. I cried out from the depths of my heart. "Jesus Christ, I believe in you. I preach about you. I think you are the Son of God. But I've never touched you. Maybe I've been indoctrinated, maybe it's all just a trick. If you are there, you know about this problem that I have. Can you help me?"[32]

Schuller goes on to further describe an encounter with "Jesus" and an accompanying vision. Those of us coming out of the New Age immediately recognize how Schuller could have unwittingly opened himself up to spiritual deception. While Schuller described what seemed to be an out of body encounter with Jesus Christ, his meditation and wavering contemplative prayer offered no assurance that the "Jesus" that purportedly spoke to him was the real Jesus (James 1:5-6; 1 John 4:1). As a matter of fact, it would not be that long before Schuller and his Crystal Cathedral would be involved with the false teachings of *A Course in Miracles*—*A Course in Miracles* whose "Jesus" said that we are all God and we are all Christ.

As a brand new Christian, I had been horrified years ago to find what amounted to be a New Age book written by a pastor and prominently displayed on the shelf of a local Christian bookstore. The book was filled with everything I had just left behind in the New Age. Cloaked in Christian language, it encouraged the reader to use guided visualization (now often called "vision casting") and other metaphysical techniques to gain whatever it was they wanted. Pastors were encouraged to "visualize and dream bigger churches," or "a new mission field," or whatever else they thought would improve their church and ministry.[33] The introduction to the book was written by Robert Schuller. In his endorsement of the book, which included these New Age visualization techniques, Schuller had written: "Don't try to understand it. Just start to enjoy it! It's true. It works. I tried it."[34]

I remember warning the bookstore owner that this book, with Schuller's extremely undiscerning endorsement, could expose countless numbers of pastors and believers to a deceptive spirit world that was only too happy to masquerade behind the labels of "God" and "Jesus" and the "Holy Spirit." She immediately removed the book from the shelf. This was one of my first clues that Robert Schuller's lack of spiritual discernment could prove to be a possible danger to those who trusted in his ministry.

But Bernie Siegel wasn't the only New Age leader praising one of Schuller's books. Neale Donald Walsch, the current point man for the New Age and the New Spirituality, had also gone way out of his way to praise Robert Schuller and to positively cite one of Schuller's books. In his 2002 book, *The New Revelations: A Conversation with God*, Walsch and his "God" used Schuller to help make their case for a world peace based on the "self-esteem" principles of a New Spirituality. Walsch favorably quoted Schuller's call for a new "theology of self-esteem" and the need for a "new reformation" within the Church.[35] The Schuller book that they had praised and were quoting from, *Self-Esteem: The New Reformation*, was the same book that Rick Warren seemed to have drawn so heavily from in referencing his remarks about "hope" and "purpose" to Bernie Siegel.

Under the circumstances, it seemed like a good time to take a closer look at the New Spirituality that Walsch and his "God" were proposing, and how they were convinced that Robert Schuller could help them achieve their purpose.

Chapter 6

The New Age PEACE Plan

The era of the Single Savior is over.[1]
Neale Donald Walsch's "God"
The New Revelations: A Conversation with God, 2002

One year after the events of September 11th, 2001, New Age leader Neale Donald Walsch's new book *The New Revelations: A Conversation with God* was published. In this book Walsch announced that "God" was now offering humanity an opportunity to avert self-destruction and achieve world peace by accepting the principles of his New Spirituality. Walsch explained that "God" was proposing a post-September 11th "PEACE Plan" that would help to bring the world's widely varying religions and belief systems closer together. Walsch's "God" was calling his PEACE Plan "The Five Steps to Peace." And both Walsch and his "God" were citing Robert Schuller as the kind of "extraordinary minister" who could help make the PEACE Plan and the New Spirituality work for everyone.

Walsch's "God" quoted a statement that Schuller had made in his 1982 book, *Self-Esteem: The New Reformation.* Schuller had written that "theologians must have their international, universal, transcreedal, transcultural, transracial standard."[2] Walsch's "God" suggested that this universal standard be the statement: "We Are All One."[3] Prior to Walsch and his "God" bringing Schuller into their conversation, they discussed their thoughts about the PEACE Plan and the world's need for a New Spirituality.

In his introduction to *The New Revelations: A Conversa-*

tion with God, Walsch wrote:

> The world is in trouble. Bigger trouble than it has ever been in before.
>
> This book provides an explanation of the crisis we are facing in a way that not only clarifies the crisis, but clarifies *how to resolve it*.[4]
>
> This is a life-altering book. It contains New Revelations. It provides the tools with which to pull ourselves *out* of despair, lifting the whole human race to a new level of experience, to a new understanding of itself, to a new expression of its grandest vision.[5]

"God" told Walsch that people are not being terrorized by other people. They are being terrorized by people's "beliefs."[6] In language and a tone reminiscent of the serpent in the Garden of Eden, Walsch's "God" explained that people don't have to change their individual beliefs, they just need to "transcend" them. He said that "transcending" does not mean that you have to abandon your beliefs completely, but rather just modify and "enlarge" them.

> "Transcending" does not mean always being "other than," it means always being "larger than." Your new, larger belief system will no doubt retain some of the old—that part of the old belief system that you experience as still serving you—and so it will be a combination of the new and the old, not a rejection of the old from top to bottom.[7]

Walsch's "God," with contrived empathy, cunningly advised that most people couldn't and shouldn't abandon *all* their beliefs because it would make everything suddenly seem "wrong." It would make their scriptures and traditions seem wrong. It would make their lives seem wrong. "God" told Walsch:

In fact, you don't have to declare that you were "wrong" about anything, because you weren't. *You simply didn't have a complete understanding. You needed more information.*

Transcending current beliefs is not an outright rejection of them; it is an "adding to" them.

Now that you have more information that you can add to what you presently believe, you can enlarge your beliefs—not *completely reject* them, *enlarge* them—and move on with your lives in a new way.

A way that works.[8]

But then there is the "catch." Walsch's New Age "God" warned that the New Spirituality will necessitate a willingness to compromise. To achieve world peace, people will have to sincerely dialogue about their perceived differences and perhaps even "give up" some of their most sacredly held beliefs. "God" explained to Walsch:

> It will take an unprecedented act of courage, on a grand scale. You may have to do something virtually unknown in the annals of human history...
>
> You may have to give up some of your most sacred beliefs.[9]

[handwritten annotations: "True" "Not Wrong" "No No No No No" "Nowhere in the Bible does it say this!" "SATAN"]

Walsch's "God" explained that in the near future established religions may still retain the general nature of their individual identities. But he severely warned that a "self-centered" and "exclusivistic" belief in a personal Savior would not be conducive to a world seeking peace and harmony. In other words, he was telling Christians that, in the days of the New Spirituality, Jesus can be your friend but not your Lord and Savior. In a statement that should sober every Christian believer on the face of the earth, Walsch's "God" warned:

[handwritten annotations: "What's up with this!" "And this is straight from Satan himself" "Not our God! Warning. Beware!" "True Christians - Different God!" "Age"]

> Yet let me make something clear. The era of the Single Savior is over. What is needed now is joint action, combined effort, collective co-creation.[10]

"God" then described his solution for how humanity can learn to live together through "combined effort" and "collective co-creation." By cleverly removing the word "Age" from "New Age Spirituality," Walsch's "God" called his repackaged New Age solution the "New Spirituality."

> The world must create a New Spirituality.
>
> Not something to completely replace the old, but something to refresh it.
>
> Not something to reduce the old, but something to expand it.
>
> Not something to subvert the old, but something to support the best of it.
>
> Human spirituality is in need of refreshment.
>
> It is now time to present the world with new theological thoughts and ideas, a new spiritual model.
>
> The world must have something new to hold on to if it is to release its grip on the old. If you were in the middle of a raging stream, would you let go of a log?...
>
> Build, therefore, a bridge.[11]

Prior to directly suggesting that Robert Schuller's theology of self-esteem could be the kind of "bridge" that could help humanity transition into the New Spirituality, Walsch's "God" formally presented his 5-Step PEACE Plan. The PEACE Plan is the proposed spiritual process that will help everyone move past "outmoded" beliefs and prepare the way for the New Spirituality. Walsch posted The Five Steps To Peace—using the word PEACE as an acronym—on his "Conversations with God" website:

THE FIVE STEPS TO PEACE

Peace will be attained when we, as human beings...

P ERMIT ourselves to acknowledge that some of our old beliefs about God and about Life are no longer working.

E XPLORE the possibility that there is something we do not understand about God and about Life, the understanding of which could change everything.

A NNOUNCE that we are willing for new understandings of God and Life to now be brought forth, understandings that could produce a new way of life on this planet.

C OURAGEOUSLY examine these new understandings and, if they align with our personal inner truth and knowing, to **enlarge** our belief system to include them.

E XPRESS our lives as a demonstration of our highest beliefs, rather than as a denial of them.[12] (Emphasis added)

The Jabez Temptation?

By using the key word "enlarge" in the fourth step of the PEACE Plan and throughout their "conversation," Walsch and his "God" seem to be making an obvious overture to the millions of Christians familiar with the first line of the prayer of Jabez (1 Chronicles 4:10) popularized by Bruce Wilkinson's best-selling book *The Prayer of Jabez*:

Oh, that You would bless me indeed, and **enlarge** my territory...[13] (Emphasis added)

Just as the word "enlarge" is central to the prayer of Jabez, so the word "enlarge" is central to the New Age PEACE Plan and the New Spirituality. Walsch and his "God" contend that everything in the world could be changed instantly for the better, if everyone—including Christians— would allow God to bless them by "enlarging" the "territory" of what they believe.

Emphasizing that key word "enlarge," and using a 5-Step format similar to the 12-Step Program of Alcoholics Anonymous, Walsch's "God" has tempted the world, and particularly the Church, to push past the constraining "boundaries"[14] of familiar doctrinal belief and accept the "huge New Truth"[15] of the New Spirituality—"We Are All One."

Later, Walsch initiated a discussion with his "God" about "Oneness," "self-esteem," and "Robert Schuller," by referring to God as the "Force" in a unified "force field."

> Such as the idea that there is, in fact, only one force field. That there is only one energy. That this is the energy of Life Itself, and that it is this energy that some people call God.[16]

Walsch's "God" explained how the world could be changed if people recognized the "Oneness" of this unified "force field" called "God."

> The simple awareness that you are all One—One with God and One with each other—and the creation of behavioral codes and international agreements reflecting that awareness, would shift the political, economic, and spiritual reality on Earth in ways that the teachings of your present day exclusivist religions can never do.
>
> This is why, if you wish to change your world as you say that you do, you are invited to now create a New Spirituality, based on New Revelations. For your old exclusivist religions and your elitist, separatist theologies no longer serve you.
>
> Not only do your biggest, most powerful organized religions teach you that you are separate from each other, they also teach you that you are not worthy of God. They teach you that you are shameful, guilty creatures; that you were born in sin and do not deserve to be the dust under God's feet. They rob you of your self-esteem.[17]

Immediately following up on the reference to "self-esteem" in relation to the New Spirituality, Neale Donald Walsch suddenly introduced Robert Schuller and Schuller's 1982 book about self-esteem into the conversation.

Robert Schuller and the New Spirituality

Walsch described Schuller as an "extraordinary minister" whose spiritual ideas are very compatible with the New Spirituality. Walsch and his "God" were very pleased and encouraged that Schuller has already proposed a "new reformation" of the Church that would be based on the principles of a "new theology" of self-esteem.[18] In praising Schuller, Walsch actually quoted from Schuller's 1982 book, *Self-Esteem: The New Reformation.* Walsch wrote:

> This extraordinary minister also declared, "As a Christian, a theologian, and a churchman within the Reformed tradition, I must believe that it is possible for the church to exist even though it may be in serious error in substance, strategy, style or spirit." But, he said, ultimately "theologians must have their international, universal, transcreedal, transcultural, transracial standard."[19]

Walsch's "God" replied:

> Rev. Schuller was profoundly astute in his observations and incredibly courageous in making them public. *I hope he is proud of himself!*

> I suggest that such an international, universal, transcreedal, transcultural, transracial standard for theology is the statement: "We Are All One. Ours is not a better way, ours is merely another way."

> This can be the gospel of a New Spirituality. It can be a kind of spirituality that gives people back to themselves.[20]

I remember reading those remarks about Schuller in *The New Revelations: A Conversation with God* when it came out in the fall of 2002. I had never taken Robert Schuller very seriously in the past, but in light of these statements by Walsch and his "God," I realized I should probably re-examine my position. Walsch and his "God" had just declared, "The era of the Single Savior is over," yet they were citing Schuller as someone whose ideas seemed to be generally compatible with their own. They were favorably comparing Schuller's call for a "new theology," and a "new reformation" of the Christian Church, to their call for a New Spirituality. *New Age / world Religion*

When I first read their remarks about Schuller I wondered how Schuller might become a part of all of this, but I couldn't imagine how. Although he tried to portray himself as an "evangelical" minister, many Bible-believing Christians were extremely suspicious of Schuller and his liberal teachings. It was hard to see how Schuller could ever have the influence necessary to convince Bible-believing Christians to accept a "new theology." *New Age Theology*

What irony that Rick Warren's book *The Purpose-Driven Life* had finally driven me to buy Schuller's book *Self-Esteem: The New Reformation*. Because Schuller seemed to have such an obvious influence on Rick Warren, and Rick Warren was so obviously influencing millions of people, I knew that I had better read the book. But when I bought it I had no idea that this 1982 Schuller book, which Neale Donald Walsch and his "God" had referred to in praising Schuller, would contain material about "hoping" and "coping" and "purpose" that would surface twenty years later in Rick Warren's *The Purpose-Driven Life*. Why was this seemingly outdated Schuller book suddenly showing up in Neale Donald Walsch's and Rick Warren's 2002 publications?

While I was surprised that Rick Warren was relying on Robert Schuller for some of his material, I was not at all surprised that the New Age would find Schuller's beliefs compatible with their own. In 1994, I had received information that had underlined Schuller's affection for New Age teachings. I was shown that Robert Schuller and his Crystal Cathedral had at one time been involved with New Age leader Jerry Jampolsky and the New Age teachings of *A Course in Miracles*. As previously mentioned, it was Jerry Jampolsky who had introduced me to *A Course in Miracles* and catalyzed my deeper involvement in New Age teachings. Ironically, Jampolsky was introducing me to the teachings of *A Course in Miracles* about the same time that Robert Schuller was introducing Jampolsky to his *Hour of Power* television audience.

With Schuller's writings and teachings suddenly being spotlighted in both the New Spirituality and the Purpose-Driven Church, I reflected for a moment on my past interaction with the Crystal Cathedral.

The Crystal Cathedral and
A Course in Miracles

On a 1994 radio broadcast, I had used the Crystal Cathedral's association with Jerry Jampolsky and *A Course in Miracles* during the early to mid-1980s as an example of how New Age teachings were starting to sneak into the Church. I outlined the deceptive teachings of *A Course in Miracles* and then commented on how the undiscerning Schuller had featured the New Age leader Jampolsky on his *Hour of Power* television program.[21] I was also aware that Course in Miracles study groups had met on Crystal Cathedral grounds, and that Cathedral staff were directing interested callers to a local Course in Miracles distribution center to purchase copies of *A Course in Miracles*.

A radio listener had been so upset at what I was reporting, she contacted the Crystal Cathedral to inquire about their position on *A Course in Miracles*. A Cathedral staff person had written a letter back to her that completely distanced Schuller and the Crystal Cathedral from the teachings of *A Course in Miracles*. The listener, in turn, forwarded the Crystal Cathedral response to the radio station as if to disprove what I had reported. That letter was then sent on to me by the station. The following is excerpted from the March 10, 1994 letter sent to the inquiring listener by the Crystal Cathedral's "Minister of Caring":

> Thank you for your letter and question. We do not believe the Course in Miracles to be a Christian course. According to the study we have done on it, while they use spiritual terms, including the name of Jesus, their basic tenants are not compatible with orthodox Christian beliefs. They do not accept Jesus Christ as the Only Son of God, the Only way to the Father, nor do they believe in the Trinity, Father, Son and Holy Spirit as being the divine three in one....

> We believe the Bible is the final revealed Word of God, and that sin and atonement are forgiven and bestowed only through a personal repentance and acceptance of Jesus Christ as one's Lord and Savior. We do not believe that we can create our own reality by "overcoming our illusory world view."

> I trust that this clears up any misunderstanding which you may have about the basic beliefs of the Hour of Power and it's differences from the Course in Miracles.[22]

Although the letter may have expressed the current 1994 position of the Crystal Cathedral Ministries, it did not address Schuller's previous involvement with Jampolsky and *A Course in Miracles*. Because it was important for all concerned that the matter be clarified, I spoke personally with the Crystal Cathedral Minister of Caring.

In our conversation she denied any Crystal Cathedral

involvement with *A Course in Miracles* at any time, including the period I referred to. Because she seemed legitimately in the dark about what had taken place, I shared additional information with her that I had not shared on my radio show. I told her that Course in Miracles study groups had met on Cathedral grounds, and I even gave her the general room locations.

In a subsequent conversation, the Cathedral representative said that she had found out I had been correct. Course in Miracles study groups *had* met at the Crystal Cathedral, but she assured me they were no longer involved with *A Course in Miracles* in any way. She seemed very nice and appeared to be genuinely unaware of the Cathedral's previous involvement with the Course. She allowed me to send her a copy of my book *The Light that was Dark*.

In a follow-up letter dated April 29, 1994, she acknowledged my book and how so many ministers were naïve about the teachings of *A Course in Miracles*. She said she had even taught a class on cults the previous year that had included warnings about "the dangers of this course." She wrote:

> Thank you so much for sending me your excellent book. I just finished reading it as I returned from the East Coast. I am so anxious to share it with many others. I do like the fact that the book is written in such a way that a person who is involved with any of the cults or metaphysical religions can read it from the beginning without being threatened. The clear description of your sincere search for spiritual peace and fulfillment I think parallels the path of many who are caught up in the deceits of Satan.
>
> I do wish I had known about the book and you last year as I taught on the cults, including the "Course in Miracles." I would really appreciate your continued prayers that God would open the eyes of those who are involved in the ministry to the dangers of this course. I continue to be

concerned at the naivete of so many.

I will keep your offer in mind to share your story and perhaps we can find a suitable time for it in the future. It is my prayer that I, and this ministry, will be used to draw confused persons to a personal relationship with Jesus Christ.

We applaud your work with the homeless, and will be praying God's continued blessings and guidance on your lives. Thank you again for sharing your story with me.[23]

And that was pretty much the end of it. I accepted her word that Schuller and his staff were no longer involved with *A Course in Miracles*. Given her strong warnings about the Course, I do remember thinking that Schuller would have served the purposes of the Lord much better if he had someone like his Minister of Caring as his *Hour of Power* guest that day instead of Jerry Jampolsky. But Schuller and his guests never seemed to talk about spiritual deception.

All of this came streaming back to me as I was suddenly being reintroduced to Robert Schuller through the writings of Neale Donald Walsch and Rick Warren. It was somewhat startling that Schuller's book *Self-Esteem: The New Reformation* was becoming known to me so many years after it was originally published. As I continued reading *Self-Esteem: The New Reformation*, I discovered that Schuller cited Gerald Jampolsky several times in his book. In one section of the book, he praised the New Age leader for his "profound theology." Schuller had written:

I am indebted to Dr. Gerald Jampolsky, a guest on our "Hour of Power," for helping me to see what is not only great psychology, but is profound theology. Obviously, there can be no conflict in truth—when psychology is "right on" and theology is "right on," there will be harmony and both shall be led to higher levels of enlightenment. "The two basic emotions," Dr. Jampolsky said, "are love and fear." Fear, then, is another word for lack of love, lack of self-love, i.e., low self-esteem.[24]

As I thought about all of this, I was struck with a curious thought. How ironic that years ago, when eager students gathered together in Crystal Cathedral classrooms to study the principles of *A Course in Miracles*, pastors who had flown in from around the world were meeting with Schuller on those same Cathedral grounds to study the principles of "successful church leadership"—pastors who thought that Schuller knew what he was doing because he had a big "successful" church and they wanted one, too. Pastors like Rick Warren.

Chapter 7

What Force Drives Your Life?

The Eternal Creative Force of the universe
we call God can surge within your being
to give you self-belief, self-esteem, self-love,
self-confidence! Without it—you're sunk,
with it—you're invincible![1]

Robert Schuller
Discover Your Possibilities, 1978

Yes, people who are spiritually and emotionally
connected to the Eternal Creative Force
discover their powerful potential as a creative
personality and win the big prize in living.[2]

Robert Schuller
If It's Going to Be, It's Up to Me, 1997

What is the basic, driving force in life?[3]

Robert Schuller
Self-Love, 1969

What is the driving force in your life?[4]

Rick Warren
The Purpose-Driven Life, 2002

Chapter Three of Rick Warren's book *The Purpose-Driven Life* is entitled "What Drives Your Life?" He began the chapter by saying:

Everyone's life is driven by something.

Most dictionaries define the verb *drive* as "to guide, to control, or to direct." Whether you are driving a car, a nail, or a golf ball, you are guiding, controlling, and directing it at that moment. What is the driving force in your life?[5]

While Rick Warren was technically correct in saying that "most dictionaries" define the verb "drive" as "to guide, control, or to direct," I found his definition far down the list in all the dictionaries I consulted. In *Webster's Dictionary*, the first four definitions of the word "drive" all had to do with the word "force."[6] The very first definition was "to force to go." A quick check in *Strong's Concordance of the Bible* and *Vine's Expository Dictionary* confirmed that all of the Bible's direct references to the word "drive" or "driven" had to do with the idea of being moved by "force."

Rick Warren acknowledged this implied meaning of "force" in the word "drive" by asking the question, "What is the driving force in your life?" He was clearly suggesting that, at least metaphorically, everyone's life is "driven" by some "force." While it may seem a little odd or even picky to put so much emphasis on the word "force," it really isn't. The word "force" is a key New Age concept and is at the heart of New Age belief. In my book *Reinventing Jesus Christ*, I had a whole sidebar in Chapter Ten on the New Age use of the word "force."

The New Age Force

Christians, especially Christian leaders, need to be very careful about their use of this word—and any word— that has such special meaning in the New Age and in the New Spirituality. One of the main ways that the New Spirituality is sneaking into the Church is through this kind of overlapping vocabulary, where Christians unknowingly use words that are heavy in New Age meaning. Words like "force."

Rick Warren highly recommended and wrote the Foreword to Erwin McManus's book entitled *An Unstoppable Force: Daring To Become The Church God Had In Mind.* In a section of his book entitled "Choose Your Words Carefully," McManus had written insightfully about the ways in which we all need to be very sensitive to how a particular word can have different meanings to different people. He had given an excellent example of the confusion that can result when people are not aware of the multiple meanings of a particular word they are using.[7] Yet, he walked right into the situation he was warning others to avoid when he described today's Church as an "unstoppable force."

Describing the Church as a "force" plays right into the New Age meaning of the word "force." And Rick Warren's question falls in the same category when he asked, "What is the driving force in your life?" The use of overlapping New Age words can create great confusion about what is really being said, and can easily lead to great deception down the line. Specific definitions of words are so very important. As petty as it might seem now, introducing crossover New Age/new gospel terms into the Church without warning about the New Age implications of these words can open the door into the New Spirituality. I had learned while in the New Age that the "God" of the New Age is often referred to as a "Force." In *Reinventing Jesus Christ*, I gave examples:

> The "God" of the "new gospel" asks Neale Donald Walsch, "What if I am not a 'man' at all, but rather, a Force?" The "Christ" of *A Course in Miracles* states that there is an "irresistible Force" within each person. Marianne Williamson explains that this "universal force" can be "activated" within each person and has "the power to make all things right." The "new gospel Christ" tells Barbara Marx Hubbard that on the day of "Planetary Pentecost" a "planetary

smile" will flash across the face of all mankind; that an "uncontrollable joy" that he describes as the "joy of the force" will "ripple" through the one body of humanity.[8]

When I became a believer, I found it very interesting that the *King James Bible* describes Antichrist as honoring the "God of forces." The prophet Daniel, looking to the "latter days," wrote this about the Antichrist:

> But in his estate shall he honour the God of forces...
> (Daniel 11:38)

It is also worth noting that Maitreya, a false New Age "Christ" and Antichrist prototype who claims to be here on Earth right now, is quoted as saying:

> Many around Me now have recognized Me, work with Me and channel My Force.[9]
>
> I am with you as the Embodiment of that Divine Force which you call the Christ Principle.[10]
>
> Many now are awake to these divine aspects, and call for the restructuring of your world.
>
> My Force is behind them.[11]

As previously mentioned, just prior to their discussion about how Robert Schuller's "new reformation" and "theology of self-esteem" could nicely dovetail with their New Spirituality, Neale Donald Walsch and his "God" discussed how God is a "force field." Walsch stated:

> Such as the idea that there is, in fact, only one force field. That there is only one energy. That this is the energy of Life Itself, and that it is this energy that some people call God.[12]

It is especially unfortunate when ministers like Robert Schuller play into the hands of the New Age/new gospel scenario and lend themselves to the purposes of the New Spirituality by referring to God as a "Force" (see Schuller quotes at the beginning of this chapter). Schuller sounded like Neale Donald Walsch when he claimed that Jesus taught the "Kingdom of God" is a "Force" within each person:

> He proclaimed these powerful words: "The Kingdom of God is within you." (Luke 17:21) This means that there's an Eternal Creative Force within you.[13]

In *If It's Going to Be, It's Up to Me*, Schuller referred to the "Eternal Creative Force" that he calls "God" as "the Divine Drive" that works within each person to give them "purpose." To underline that God is this "Force" or "Divine Drive" that works through everyone giving them "purpose," he quoted Philippians 2:13:

> "It is God at work in me giving me the *will* and the power to achieve His purpose"...[14] (Translation unspecified)

Schuller's references to God being the "Force" and "Divine Drive" working within each person to achieve God's "purpose" had given a definite implied New Age meaning to Schuller's use of the word "purpose." It also had given implied New Age meaning to the question he asked his readers in his 1969 book *Self-Love*: "What is the basic, driving force in life?" Considering Rick Warren's inclination to use unattributed Schuller material, one cannot assume that his similarly-worded question 33 years later does not carry some of Schuller's implied New Age meaning when he also asked: "What is the driving force in your life?"

Especially in light of all we know about the New Age meaning attached to the word "force," asking the question

"What is the driving force in your life?" is probably not the best way to approach anyone. The very question demands that your answer be necessarily defined as some kind of "force." If Christians answer that God is the driving "force" in their life they have just defined their God in New Age/new gospel terms. It is important that Christians understand what the New Age and the New Spirituality mean when they use the word "force." It is confusing when pastors like Robert Schuller, Rick Warren, and Erwin McManus use the word indiscriminately and with no explanation.

The word "force" can be one of those overlapping terms that starts to blur the line between traditional Christianity and the New Spirituality. So, while Robert Schuller and Rick Warren ask their readers, "What is the driving force in your life?" readers should in turn be asking them to please provide some definitions and make some distinctions between their use and the New Age use of the word "force."

Chapter 8

God is in Everything?

The Bible says, "*He rules everything and is everywhere and is in everything.*" [1]
Rick Warren
The Purpose-Driven Life, 2002

Yes, God is alive and He is in every single human being! [2]
Robert Schuller
Hour of Power, November 9, 2003

God is in everyone and everything. [3]
Bernie Siegel
Prescriptions for Living, 1999

When I got to page 88 in *The Purpose-Driven Life*, I stared at Rick Warren's words in amazement. He had written:

> Because God is with you all the time, no place is any closer to God than the place where you are right now. The Bible says, "*He rules everything and is everywhere and is in everything.*"

God is *in* everything? Rick Warren seemed to be teaching what I had been taught by my New Age teachers and teachings: that God was "in" everyone and everything. I wondered which one of his many Bible versions had told him that. His footnote told me that the Ephesians 4:6 scripture he was citing came from a Bible entitled the *New Century*

Version. I had never heard of it before, but I later found it prominently advertised on the first page of a current Robert Schuller website.[4] I also noticed that Rick Warren's name was mentioned on the same page as the *New Century Version* ad. In a column describing an upcoming church growth conference at his Institute for Successful Church Leadership, Schuller had written:

You're Invited to Discover a Fantastic
New Dream for Your Church!

The theme for the 2004 Robert H. Schuller Institute for Successful Church Leadership is, If You Can Dream It You Can Do It! Dare to dream that your church can overcome, can succeed, and can make a difference in your community and in your world today.

Is your church all God wants it to be? Send your pastors and lay church leaders to the 34th Robert H. Schuller Institute for Successful Church Leadership; which brings together the most prominent pastors who make faith come alive in some of the country's largest churches, like Bill Hybels of Willow Creek Community Church, and Rick Warren of Saddleback Church, both graduates of the Institute.

I hadn't been aware of the fact that Rick Warren was a graduate of the Schuller Institute and that he also taught there. Knowing this helped me to understand the heavy Schuller influence I was discovering in *The Purpose-Driven Life*. Within weeks of reading Rick Warren's statement that God was "in" everything, I discovered that Robert Schuller was saying pretty much the same thing. In an *Hour of Power* sermon he had proudly proclaimed:

Yes, God is alive and He is in every single human being![5] (Emphasis in original)

What I would later find out, in my related Schuller reading, was that Schuller had been teaching this New Age doctrine of "Immanence"—that God is "in" everyone—for many years. For example, in his 1969 book, *Self-Love*, Schuller had written:

God lives in people.[6] *IF you know his Son Jesus*

Purpose Driven Course in Miracles

Rick Warren's implication and Robert Schuller's contention that God is "in" every person is at the very heart of all New Age thinking. The Bible does *not* teach this. The *New Century Version* that Rick Warren quotes is dangerously mistaken in its translation of Ephesians 4:6. The only books I had ever seen that taught that God was "in" everything had nothing to do with biblical Christianity. In fact, it didn't take me long to find this same unbiblical teaching in *A Course in Miracles*. The word "purpose" was curiously prevalent throughout the teaching. I read the lesson heading shown below from *A Course in Miracles*, and then noted what followed:

Lesson 29
God is in everything I see.

The idea for today explains why you can see all **purpose** in everything. It explains why nothing is separate, by itself or in itself....

And what shares the **purpose** of the universe shares the **purpose** of its Creator....

Nothing is as it appears to you. Its holy **purpose** stands beyond your little range.[7] (Emphasis added)

The *New Century Version*, quoted by Rick Warren, was teaching what *A Course in Miracles* and my other New Age books had taught me years ago—that God is "in" everyone and everything. It completely misrepresents what the Apostle Paul was actually stating in Ephesians 4:6. In this scripture Paul is not writing to the world at large. The book of Ephesians is Paul's letter to the Church of Ephesus and to the faithful followers of Jesus Christ. In Ephesians 1:1 he makes it clear that he is writing to "the saints which are at Ephesus, and to the faithful in Christ Jesus."

According to properly translated Scripture, God is not "in" everyone and everything. God's Holy Spirit is *only* sent to those who truly accept Jesus Christ as their Lord and Savior (John 14:15-17; Acts 5:32). Because the Church of Ephesus was composed of believers who had accepted Jesus as their Lord and Savior, God had sent His Holy Spirit to them. Therefore, as a result of their conversion God's Holy Spirit resided in them all. Thus, Paul is *only* addressing the *believers* of Ephesus and the "faithful in Christ Jesus" when he stated that God is "above all, and through all, and in *you* all" (emphasis added). He was not saying that God is present in unbelievers. He was not saying that God is "in" everyone and "in" everything. That is what the New Age teaches. Compare Ephesians 4:6 in the *New Century Version* that Rick Warren quoted with the *King James Bible*:

> "*He rules everything and is everywhere and is in everything.*" (NCV)[8]

One God and Father of all, who is above all, and through all, and in **you** all. (*King James Bible*; emphasis added)

The "you" in the *King James Bible* makes it very clear that Paul is writing his letter to the *believers* who are in the Church of Jesus Christ. He is not writing to those who are unbelievers, and who just happen to be reading his letter. He is certainly not saying or suggesting that God is "in" everyone and everything. But the New Age teachers with their New Spirituality are trying to co-opt this scripture to make it apply to the whole human race. And many of today's newer Bible versions, like some of the ones Robert Schuller and Rick Warren are using, seem to justify this New Age interpretation. By choosing the *New Century Version*, Rick Warren is actually giving the New Age exactly what it wants—apparent scriptural authority for their key New Age teaching that "we are all One" because God is "in" everyone and everything.

Why would Rick Warren pick a Bible version that seems to legitimize the New Spirituality's doctrine of "Oneness?" Ironically, in *From the Ashes: A Spiritual Response to the Attack on America*, Neale Donald Walsch had challenged Rick Warren and Christian leaders everywhere to accept the new gospel that "We are all One" because God is "in" everyone and everything. However, instead of refuting this New Age teaching and contending for the faith, Rick Warren chose a Bible version that makes it appear he is actually agreeing with Walsch's doctrine of "Oneness."

New Age leader and Global Renaissance Alliance member Wayne Dyer is a good example of how Rick Warren's teaching that God "is everywhere and is in everything" is being used for the New Age purposes of the New Spirituality. In an interview in the September 2004 issue of *Science of Mind* magazine, Dyer stated:

> The interesting thing is that if you accept that God is everywhere—that this Source is everywhere—that means that there's nowhere that it is not. So first of all, you have to accept that it is within you...If it's everywhere, and it's in you...all you have to do is realign yourself in such a way so you can reconnect yourself to that thing to which you're already connected.[9]

Oneness with the New Age?

B ecause Rick Warren placed such great emphasis on Eugene Peterson's *The Message*, I looked up Ephesians 4:6 in *The Message*. Peterson's paraphrase also definitely lends itself to the New Age interpretation that God is present "in" everyone. He also introduces his readers—with no parenthetical warnings or explanations—to the concept of "Oneness":

> You have one Master, one faith, one baptism, one God and Father of all, who rules over all, works through all, and is present in all. Everything you are and think and do is permeated with Oneness.[10]

When I was involved in New Age teachings and studying *A Course in Miracles*, I was taught that the concept of "Oneness" is inextricably linked to the understanding that God is "in" everything. As I looked at two specific quotes from *A Course in Miracles*, I saw the obvious similarity between its teachings and the Ephesians 4:6 translations being presented to the Church by Robert Schuller, Rick Warren, Eugene Peterson and others. The Course stated:

> God is in everything I see.[11]

> The oneness of the Creator and the creation is your wholeness, your sanity and your limitless power.[12]

Maitreya, the false Christ who claims he is already here on Earth, also presents this New Age foundational doctrine of Oneness.

> My friends, God is nearer to you than you can imagine.
> God is yourself.
> God is within you and all around you.[13]

I am All in All.[14]

My name is Oneness.[15]

New age author Bernie Siegel, who is so nonchalantly cited by both Rick Warren and Robert Schuller in their writings, also teaches this key New Age doctrine.

God is in everyone and everything.[16]

God is all.[17]

In his book *Friendship with God*, Walsch quoted his "God" as telling him:

> The twenty-first century will be the time of awakening, of meeting The Creator Within. Many beings will experience Oneness with God and with all of life. This will be the beginning of the golden age of the New Human, of which it has been written; the time of the universal human, which has been eloquently described by those with deep insight among you.
>
> There are many such people in the world now—teachers and messengers, Masters and visionaries—who are placing this vision before humankind and offering tools with which to create it. These messengers and visionaries are the heralds of a New Age.[18]

Doctrinal Leaven

In Galatians 5:9, the Bible warns: "A little leaven leaveneth the whole lump." Jesus warned His disciples to beware of the doctrinal leaven that was being introduced by their religious leaders (Matthew 16:12). In choosing to use a poor Bible translation of Ephesians 4:6, Rick Warren is introducing New Age leaven into the Church. If the Church accepts Rick Warren's teaching that God is present "in" everything, then it is only a hop, skip and a jump to the doctrine of Oneness and the New Spirituality. "A little leaven leaveneth the whole lump."

The Bible, when properly translated, makes it very clear that we are *not* "One" because God is *not* "in" everyone and everything. We are only "one" through the person of Jesus Christ when we truly accept Him as our Lord and Savior:

Amen

> For ye are all the children of God by faith in Christ Jesus. For as many of you as have been baptized into Christ have put on Christ. There is neither Jew nor Greek, there is neither bond nor free, there is neither male nor female: for ye are all one in Christ Jesus. (Galatians 3:26-28)

Thus, the Holy Spirit of God is sent to indwell believers who have accepted Jesus Christ as their Lord and Savior. It is important to note that this does not mean believers are "God" or in any way divine. God's Word makes this point very clear—man is *not* God (Ezekiel 28:2; Isaiah 45:18-23).

Time to Revisit Schuller and Jampolsky

Rick Warren's use of Ephesians 4:6 from the *New Century Version* that declares God is "in" everything was extremely troubling. Amazingly, he seemed oblivious to the New Age implications of what he was teaching, which was strangely reminiscent of Robert Schuller, Jerry Jampolsky and *A Course in Miracles*. Schuller has obviously been a strong influence on Rick Warren, so was this teaching on Ephesians 4:6 something that Rick Warren had picked up from him? It was at this point I decided to revisit Robert Schuller and his involvement with Jerry Jampolsky and the New Age teachings of *A Course in Miracles*. Something didn't seem right about all of this, and I needed some answers. Over the coming months in a number of different ways I would definitely get those answers.

Chapter 9

Robert Schuller and
Jerry Jampolsky

**Then he [Jampolsky] became a believer in God.
That's a long story.**[1]
Robert Schuller
Legacy of Hope Video, 1996

It was becoming obvious that Robert Schuller was much more influential than I had ever imagined. Neale Donald Walsch and his New Age "God" were citing him favorably, and his overriding influence with Rick Warren was becoming more and more apparent as I continued my reading of *The Purpose-Driven Life.*

Realizing I had to take Schuller much more seriously, I proceeded to revisit his previous involvement with Jerry Jampolsky and the New Age teachings of *A Course in Miracles.* Curious, but not really expecting to find anything recent, I put the names of Robert Schuller and Jerry Jampolsky into the search engine of the computer. As I did, I remembered the 1994 letter I had received from the Crystal Cathedral representative assuring me that the Crystal Cathedral was no longer involved with *A Course in Miracles* and that they were now exposing the Course as a false teaching. So I was more than a little surprised when a Schuller sermon with Jampolsky's name and a 2003 copyright date popped up on the computer screen. It was entitled "Become A Peace Maker."[2] Was it possible Schuller was still talking about Jampolsky? In this particular sermon, appearing on his *Hour of Power* website, Schuller discussed Jesus' beatitude, "Blessed are the peacemakers: for they shall be called the children of God" (Matthew 5:9). New Age leader Jampolsky was Schuller's first example of a "Peace Maker."

Schuller introduced Jampolsky as "[o]ne of the many psychiatrists, with whom I have a very respected relationship." He praised Jampolsky for his "profound understanding" that "The Opposite of Love is Not Hate! The Opposite of Love is FEAR." He went on to relate an incident that Jampolsky described in his book *Love Is Letting Go of Fear*. In his praise of Jampolsky, Schuller neglected to mention that Jampolsky had found "God" through the teachings of *A Course in Miracles*, and that the book he was indirectly referring to—*Love Is Letting Go of Fear*—was completely based on the teachings of *A Course in Miracles*. On the dedication page of *Love Is Letting Go of Fear*, Jampolsky had written for Schuller and all of his readers to see:

> This book is dedicated to Helen and Bill, who have been both teachers and friends to me. It was because of their joint willingness that *A Course in Miracles* came into being, a work which provides the foundation for this book.[3]

For those not familiar with *A Course in Miracles* (see Chapter One of my book, *Reinventing Jesus Christ: The New Gospel*[4]), here are some of the New Age teachings presented in this set of books that are so diametrically opposed to the teachings of the Bible, yet so highly recommended by Jerry Jampolsky:

> Do not make the pathetic error of "clinging to the old rugged cross."[5]

> The journey to the cross should be the last "useless journey."[6]

The recognition of God is the recognition of yourself.[7]

When God created you He made you part of Him.[8]

There is no sin; it has no consequence.[9]

The Atonement is the final lesson he [man] need learn, for it teaches him that, never having sinned, he has no need of salvation.[10]

For Christ takes many forms with different names until their oneness can be recognized.[11]

In the "Author's Note" of *Love Is Letting Go of Fear,* Jampolsky gives his personal testimony of how he found God and inner peace through the teachings of *A Course in Miracles.* His book is short, simple, and very appealing to an undiscerning reader. It was this little book that led me to *A Course in Miracles* and catalyzed my deeper involvement in New Age teachings.

It was the process of describing my own involvement with Jampolsky's book and *A Course in Miracles* on that 1994 radio program that had prompted my comment about Schuller's involvement with Jampolsky and the Course. As previously mentioned in Chapter Six, I had used Schuller as an example of how New Age teachings were sneaking into the Church. Those comments had resulted in the Crystal Cathedral originally denying any involvement with the Course. Then came their admission that Course in Miracles groups had indeed met at the Crystal Cathedral but that the Cathedral was no longer doing groups or involved in any way with the Course.

But if the Crystal Cathedral had really distanced itself from Jerry Jampolsky and *A Course in Miracles,* why was this sermon with a reference to Jampolsky showing up with a 2003 *Hour of Power* copyright? Was Schuller still talking about Jampolsky, or had some staff person made a mistake and posted an old sermon? Whatever the case, I was surprised at this recent mention of Jampolsky.

Schuller's "dear friend" Jerry Jampolsky

Over the next few months, I would learn some very important and disturbing things about Schuller's involvement with Jampolsky and *A Course in Miracles*. Because of Rick Warren's involvement with Schuller, I had continued reading through a number of Schuller's books, including his 1982 book, *Self-Esteem: The New Reformation*. *Self-Esteem* was obviously a very key work, as material from this book was surfacing in the writings of both Rick Warren *and* Neale Donald Walsch. Early on in my reading of this book by Schuller, I had discovered the first of several references to Jampolsky. Schuller was quoting from 1 Corinthians 13, and he was writing about the importance of love.

> Dr. Gerald Jampolsky, a prominent American psychiatrist and head of the Center for Attitudinal Healing in Tiburon, California, who lectures before audiences from the American Psychiatric Association to television talk shows has been preaching this theme: "The two basic emotions are not love and hate, but love and fear." The opposite of love is not hate, but fear. What is fear but the absence of love? And what is the absence of love but the presence of fear?[12]

While Schuller credits these understandings about "love" and "fear" to Jampolsky, Jampolsky made it very clear in his book *Love Is Letting Go of Fear* that his teachings about "love" and "fear" come from the teachings of *A Course in Miracles*. Ironically, when Schuller was stating this basic Course understanding—"What is fear but the absence of love?" in his 1982 book *Self-Esteem: The New Reformation*—I was studying almost these exact same words in my Course in Miracles study group. In *A Course in Miracles*, the Course's counterfeit "Jesus" stated:

And what is fear except love's absence?[13]

It was becoming apparent to me why Neale Donald Walsch and his "God" were so fond of this particular Schuller book. Not only was Schuller's self-esteem theology lending itself to their New Spirituality, but Schuller was also introducing his readers to New Age leader Jerry Jampolsky and teachings that came directly from *A Course in Miracles*.

Three years later, Schuller had apparently become friends with Jampolsky. In his 1985 book, *The Be (Happy) Attitudes*, Schuller wrote:

> Dr. Gerald Jampolsky, a noted psychiatrist and a dear friend of mine, was for twenty-five years a very strong agnostic. Then one day, without warning, his life totally changed, and he became a believer in God. I asked him once when we were together, "Dr. Jampolsky, in the years before you were converted, what did you think about people who went to church?"
>
> He said, "For twenty-five years I thought people who went to church, prayed, and believed in God were not normal. I thought they were really kind of sick. Now I see that I was completely wrong. *They* were normal; I was not."[14]

But Schuller was not being straight about Jampolsky when he said, "Then one day, without warning, his life totally changed, and he became a believer in God." Jampolsky makes it very clear, in his many writings, that one day someone handed him a copy of *A Course in Miracles* and his life was totally changed as he became a believer in the "God" and "Christ" of *A Course in Miracles*. Schuller was being completely disingenuous, implying that Jerry Jampolsky has had a legitimate conversion to traditional Christianity. Jerry Jampolsky did *not* become a believer in the God and Christ of the Bible. Robert Schuller knows this. In fact, almost everything that Jampolsky has said and done since 1975 has been a personal testimony to how his life was changed by the New Age teachings of *A Course in Miracles*. In 1985, when Schuller cited Jampolsky in his book *The Be (Happy) Attitudes*, Jampolsky was by far the most popularly published and well-known proponent of *A Course in Miracles*. It was also during this same year that members of Schuller's staff were facilitating Course in Miracles groups at the Crystal Cathedral.

Because my reading of *The Purpose-Driven Life* was forcing me to take a much closer look at Robert Schuller, I called my original source concerning Schuller's involvement with *A Course in Miracles*. After our conversation, she sent me an actual copy of the notes she had made on October 3, 1985, when she had spoken on the phone with several of the secretaries at the Crystal Cathedral. Here are some direct quotes from her notes:

> Talked to several secretaries who confirmed Course being taught there... informal study group—meet Monday night—Held in one of group therapy offices... 5-6 months into reading it... 2nd year... H.S. [Holy Spirit] dictated it—fine w/ us... Miracle Distribution Center—can find books there [proceeded to give directions]—ask for Conrad Hanson who teaches our [group]... early group starts at 6—2nd group at 7:30... books cost $50... Have Jampolsky's books... Dr. Schuller [regarding *A Course in Miracles*]—"that's a wonderful book to have in your library"— (His) on bottom shelf.

> Reaches many groups—Nothing wrong w/ that... Church of Religious Science uses it—All paths lead to the same place... Fine w/ us—Occult people can use it—Truth is Truth—we can all drink from same cup... Unity Church— very close to what we're doing... we're Dutch Reform of America... Schuller more open place of study—than it is

fundamentalist—open minded campus—As long as you're
seeking truth—no one will light a cross on (your door-
step)... All are welcomed at this church... Conrad Hanson...
Head of New Hope Hotline Counseling line for 15 yrs... [is
at] Miracle Distribution Center.[15]

I called my source back, and she confirmed that I had
read her notes correctly. She had definitely been told that
Schuller had a copy of *A Course in Miracles* in his office and
that one of the Course study groups had been facilitated by
Conrad Hanson—the long time director of Schuller's New
Hope Hotline—who was apparently associated with the
nearby Miracle Distribution Center. She also confirmed that
she was told she could purchase *A Course in Miracles* at The
Miracle Distribution Center, and that she was given explicit
directions on how to get there. She said that, although her
conversation was limited to several secretaries, they seemed
very knowledgeable and quite sure of what they were
saying. I told her I was going to check to see if Conrad
Hanson was still at the Miracle Distribution Center—if the
Center was even still in business. After I got off the phone,
I called Los Angeles information and asked if they had a
number for the Miracle Distribution Center. They did. It was
still in business.

Schuller and Jampolsky
Did Workshops Together?

The next afternoon I called the Miracle Distribution
Center. A man answered the phone. I mentioned that I
had been a student of *A Course in Miracles* and was wondering if Conrad Hanson was still associated with the Center.
I was taken aback when the man on the phone told me that
he was Conrad Hanson.

We quickly entered into a general conversation about

Jerry Jampolsky, Robert Schuller and *A Course in Miracles*. He was very congenial and volunteered that Schuller had been pressured to back off from *A Course in Miracles* because of criticism from some of the more "conservative" members of his church. He then almost eagerly volunteered that the relationship between Schuller and Jampolsky had been much more involved than it appeared on the surface. He told me that Jampolsky and Schuller had actually done workshops together in Hawaii.[16]

When we finished talking, I hung up the phone amazed that he had volunteered the fact that Schuller had done workshops with Jampolsky. Schuller knew *exactly* what he was doing with Jampolsky and *A Course in Miracles* but apparently had to back off under pressure from members of his church. He was also probably feeling the increased scrutiny that was coming from Christian researchers who were starting to recognize Schuller as someone who was very sympathetic to New Age teachings. But this is where it all seemed to end. The Jerry Jampolsky and Course in Miracles trail seemed to suddenly dry up in 1985. And the Cathedral Minister of Caring I had communicated with in 1994 had assured me that the Crystal Cathedral was no longer involved with *A Course in Miracles* in any way—except to expose it as a false teaching.

But There's More to the Story...

So, the "official" position given to me was that Crystal Cathedral involvement with *A Course in Miracles* had ended in 1985. Although I never heard any more on the matter from Schuller's Minister of Caring, I had accepted her explanation that Schuller and his staff had abandoned their involvement with *A Course in Miracles*. As far as I was concerned, the whole issue had been put to rest. Thus, I assumed that the *Hour of Power* posting of the 2003 copyrighted sermon referencing Jampolsky was probably an old sermon.

But just before Christmas I went to the local Barnes and Noble bookstore to look for a gift for my wife. Finding several books I knew she would like, I was on my way to the sales desk when I spied a large, prominently displayed, video/tape/book set with Robert Schuller's face on the cover. He was standing in front of a scenic sunset, and the packaged set was entitled *Robert Schuller Presents His Legacy of Hope: The Be Happy Attitudes: Eight Positive Attitudes that can Transform Your Life.*

I was surprised that Schuller was re-releasing the book that described how his New Age "friend" Jerry Jampolsky had become "a believer in God." The back cover indicated the book was a special "gift edition" of the *Be (Happy) Attitudes.* It also included two cassette tapes and two videos that presented Schuller in a series of "warm and intimate conversations" about the book. Curious, I bought the packaged set and took it home. When I opened it up, I saw that all the materials had a 1996 copyright. I figured that he had probably deleted the part of his book about Jampolsky—but he had not. The book was exactly the same text he had written in 1985. He had let the Jampolsky anecdotes stand. But it was hard to imagine that he would mention Jampolsky on the video. I put the videotape into my VCR.

On the video, Schuller sat in a comfortable armchair in front of a fireplace, in a friendly living-room setting, surrounded by his church friends and family. Upbeat and "positive" as always, he talked about peace and love and the "Be Happy Attitudes." He shared anecdotes and elicited powerful stories from some of those in attendance as he moved through his material. Suddenly, there it was right at the beginning of the second video. Presenting Jesus' beatitude "Blessed are the pure in heart for they shall see God," Schuller used Jerry Jampolsky to illustrate a person's willingness to let God "come into your life and flow through you." He said:

> You know its been my joy to be the friend of many great psychiatrists of this century. One is Dr. Gerald Jampolsky. And He was a Jewish boy bar mitzvahed at twelve. And the next year his rabbi left the sacred calling to become a stock broker which really disillusioned this little boy. And he thinks as he analyzes it now he became an atheist at that point. He became a young atheist.
>
> He went into medical school, became a very brilliant medical doctor. But he had problems himself, as all humans do. **Then he became a believer in God. That's a long story.** But I said to him one day, I said, "Jerry, during those many years that you practiced as an atheistic psychiatrist what did you think of me and people like us who went to church?" "Oh," he said, "I thought you were not normal. People who believe in God aren't normal." He said, "Now I see it just completely the opposite. You are normal. I was not normal."
>
> Faith in God is man's natural home. But if you choose to leave that and live in the world of skepticism and unbelief and doubt, that world does not generate joy. That world does not produce personalities that are bubbling, open, enthusiastic, and happy. That world doesn't work if it doesn't produce open, transparent, emotionally healthy human personalities....You believe in God—let him flow through you. "Ah," Jampolsky says, "now you're normal."[17] (Emphasis added)

After describing Jampolsky's former atheism, Schuller stated: "Then he became a believer in God. That's a long story." You bet it is. The "God" Jampolsky found and believes in is the "God" of the New Age—*not* the God of biblical Christianity. Jampolsky would be the first one to tell you that, and Schuller knows this. More than fourteen years after Schuller had Jampolsky as his guest on the *Hour of*

Power, Robert Schuller was still portraying the New Age leader as a traditional believer in the Bible's Jesus Christ.

Jerry Jampolsky is undoubtedly a very nice man. Certainly he is a very committed and caring person. But ever since his New Age conversion in 1975, his life has been founded on the principles of *A Course in Miracles*. *A Course in Miracles* whose "Jesus" teaches that "there is no sin" and that "the journey to the cross is the last useless journey." *A Course in Miracles* that teaches there is no need for salvation from a personal Savior because we are already "One" with God. *A Course in Miracles* whose "Jesus" teaches that "Oneness" pervades everything because God is "in" everyone and everything.

When Schuller cleverly evaded disclosing Jampolsky's testimony by saying "that's a long story," he neatly sidestepped all of the New Age detail that Jampolsky has explicitly laid out in his many books and lectures. And for Schuller to still be doing this in 1996 obviously contradicted what I had been told two years prior to the taping of the video. For Schuller, at this point, to be implying that Jampolsky is a converted "Christian" betrays not only his affection for New Age teachers and teachings but reveals an obvious hypocrisy in what he has been communicating about the Christian faith. Robert Schuller is not being honest with the millions of people who put their trust in him as a minister.

Schuller and Jampolsky Today

Even as I was writing this chapter for the first edition of this book *Deceived on Purpose*, Robert Schuller once again wove Jerry Jampolsky's name into his March 28th, 2004 *Hour of Power* telecast. After referring to Jesus as the "original gentle giant," Schuller singled out Jampolsky as a modern day example of a "gentle giant."[18] Then, incredibly, on October 17, 2004, as I was preparing the second edition of this book, Jerry Jampolsky—the New Age leader who introduced me to *A Course in Miracles*—was Robert Schuller's special guest on his worldwide *Hour of Power* telecast.[19] As Schuller interviewed Jampolsky and his wife Diane on the subject of "forgiveness," hardly anyone watching would know of the New Age snags and snares that lay hidden below the surface of their seemingly "positive" remarks. With Schuller facilitating their discussion, the three of them nonchalantly introduced key words and phrases that I recognized from my previous study of *A Course in Miracles*. Yet throughout their discussion, and amidst all of Schuller's magnanimous praise for Jampolsky's work, Schuller conveniently neglected to mention that Jampolsky's "fabulous books" were founded on the New Age teachings of *A Course in Miracles*.

During this *Hour of Power* interview, Schuller spotlighted Jampolsky's International Center of Attitudinal Healing, with its 130 individual Attitudinal Healing Centers located all around the world. Those watching on television would again have no idea that Jampolsky's whole concept of "attitudinal healing" was based on the teachings of *A Course in Miracles*. The official website of the Miracle Distribution Center—the same Miracle Distribution Center that had provided *A Course in Miracles* books for Crystal Cathedral referrals back in 1985—clearly stated:

> Gerald Jampolsky is a psychiatrist who was introduced to *A Course in Miracles* in 1975. As a married couple, Jerry and Diane have worked extensively with children who have catastrophic diseases and helped them to heal their lives through **Attitudinal Healing, a form of mental healing based on the Course.**[20] (Emphasis added)

Schuller's joint appearance with Jampolsky and his wife at the Crystal Cathedral service clearly underlined the contentions of the first edition of *Deceived on Purpose* that Schuller has been less than honest about the extent of his relationship with Jampolsky and the Course. Although Schuller continues to remain strangely silent regarding the New Age foundation of Jampolsky's teachings, his recent unabashed, and almost "in your face," appearance with Jampolsky was an amazing Sign of the Times.

More than twenty-two years after Jampolsky's first guest appearance on the *Hour of Power*, Robert Schuller still obviously regards Jampolsky's Course in Miracles-based teachings and his conversion to the "God" of the New Age as something to celebrate and share with the world. And, in so doing, Schuller is revealing himself to be the kind of leader who is willing to compromise and sacrifice God's truth for the purposes of the New Age and the New Spirituality.

A quick check on Schuller's website after the interview revealed that Jampolsky's 1999 book *Forgiveness: The Greatest Healer of All* was currently available at the Crystal Cathedral bookstore.[21] The Foreword to *Forgiveness*— described by Schuller as a "fantastic" book[22]—was written by New Age leader Neale Donald Walsch.

It was becoming increasingly clear why Neale Donald Walsch and his "God" praised Robert Schuller and quoted from his 1982 book *Self-Esteem: The New Reformation*. It was now making much more sense to me why they were calling for a New Spirituality based on Schuller's "theology of self-esteem." They recognized Schuller as someone who was sympathetic to their New Age point of view, and who had the potential to transition countless numbers of people calling themselves Christians into the New Age and into the New Spirituality.

As I reflected on what was happening, I thought about the seemingly sincere Minister of Caring who assured me, back in 1994, that the Crystal Cathedral had become aware of the dangers of *A Course in Miracles*. I recalled how she had requested prayer that naive Christian ministers would have their eyes opened to the dangers of the Course. On her Crystal Cathedral letterhead she had written:

> I would really appreciate your continued prayers that God would open the eyes of those who are involved in the ministry to the dangers of this course. I continue to be concerned at the naivete of so many.[23]

Schuller and the Church Growth Movement

I remember being amazed years ago, when the pastor of a Florida church I was attending suddenly went off to one of Schuller's church growth conferences at the Crystal Cathedral. I was shocked that an apparently solid Bible-believing pastor would look to Schuller for any kind of guidance. It just seemed so strange to me that Schuller had become somewhat of a "guru" in the church growth movement. And I continue to find it almost incomprehensible that countless numbers of pastors and Christian leaders still flock to Schuller's Crystal Cathedral to learn the principles of "successful church leadership." Men, like Rick Warren, who have adopted not only Schuller's church growth principles, but his anecdotes and stories and skewed beliefs as well. Leaders who should have seen through Schuller, but apparently are more interested in "growing" their churches than in exercising spiritual discernment. Leaders who are so intent on having a "successful" church they have disregarded the warnings that have been shouted out to them from the pages of properly translated Scripture. Leaders who have perhaps looked more to Schuller for their inspiration than to their Heavenly Father.

Another New Age Testimony
for Robert Schuller

B ecause of the obvious Schuller influence that I had discovered in *The Purpose-Driven Life*, I had by now spent many hours reading the published works of Robert Schuller. His strong New Age leanings over the years had become apparent to me in a number of different ways. But none was stranger than the one that presented itself the week after I thought I had concluded writing this chapter.

I had returned to the same bookstore where I had previously purchased a number of Schuller books. With several more Schuller books in hand I proceeded over to the cash register. The worker, a friendly grey-haired woman, talked knowledgeably about Schuller and his ministry. After several minutes of general conversation, she suddenly told me that in the early 1970s she had attended the Schuller Institute for Successful Church Leadership. She said that she and her husband were Religious Science ministers, and back at that time they had just started a Church of Religious Science outside of Los Angeles.

She stated that she had gone to the Institute because she wanted their new church to grow and to be as success- ful as possible. She said that the time with Schuller and his staff was very helpful. She and her husband had applied the techniques and principles taught by Schuller, and their church had really grown. She said that she and her husband had applied these same techniques in other Religious Science churches they had ministered to over the years with similarly successful results. She volunteered that their churches had often used Schuller's books because they were so compatible with their own New Age teachings. She agreed with my observation that Schuller seemed to be providing a spiritual bridge between the teachings of traditional Christianity and the teachings of the New Age.

Then she told me that during her time at the Institute, the group had visited with Schuller in his church office. In a conversation with Schuller, she had shared with him that she was a minister with the Church of Religious Science. Acknowledging her New Age beliefs, he opened his bottom desk drawer and pulled out a copy of Religious Science founder Ernest Holmes' book *Science of Mind*. She said Schuller seemed very comfortable showing her that he had this classic New Age text.

When I left the store I told my wife that it was pretty sobering to know that the church growth movement in this country, which has trained thousands of pastors like Rick Warren, was started by a man who is so obviously drawn to New Age teachers and teachings. And, as I said that, I realized the irony of what I had just been told in the bookstore. I remembered something I had read in Rick Warren's book *The Purpose-Driven Church*. Right about the time Schuller was showing this Religious Science minister Ernest Holmes' New Age book, a young Rick Warren was reading his first Robert Schuller book on church growth and starting to put his trust in Schuller as a teacher.[24]

Thirty years later, I wondered if anything had really changed. It seemed that Robert Schuller was still drawn to New Age teachings, and it seemed that Rick Warren was still drawn to Robert Schuller. And it was in this broader context of Rick Warren's relationship to Schuller that I was able to more clearly understand the extremely serious New Age/new gospel implications of *The Purpose-Driven Life*.

Chapter 10

Robert Schuller and Rick Warren

The more I read Robert Schuller, the more I was shocked at how so many of Rick Warren's thoughts, ideas, references, words, terms, phrases, and quotes in *The Purpose-Driven Life* seemed to be directly inspired by Schuller's writings and teachings. Surprisingly, Rick Warren does not directly acknowledge Schuller in *The Purpose-Driven Life*. A generic tip of the hat to "the hundreds of writers and teachers" that "shaped" his life hardly did justice to the Schuller influence that had become so obvious in his book. An influence that went at least as far back as Rick Warren's last year in seminary.

In 1979, as a last year seminary student and a year before he started Saddleback Church, Rick Warren and his wife Kay drove all the way from Texas to California to attend one of Robert Schuller's church growth seminars. In a feature story on Rick Warren in the November 18, 2002 issue of *Christianity Today* entitled "A Regular Purpose-Driven Guy," Tim Stafford wrote:

> During his last year in seminary, he and Kay drove west to visit Robert Schuller's Institute for Church Growth. "We had a very stony ride out to the conference," she says, because such nontraditional ministry scared her to death. Schuller, though, won them over. "He had a profound influence on Rick," Kay says. "We were captivated by his positive appeal to nonbelievers. I never looked back."[2]

The article described how Rick Warren later moved to Orange County, starting his church in close proximity to Schuller's Crystal Cathedral. It was there that he started the process of building his own mega-church by directly implementing the principles and techniques he had learned from Schuller. Stafford explained:

> Imitating Schuller, Warren walked the (then unincorporated but fast-growing) town of Lake Forest, asking what kept people from going to church.[3]

The young pastor, continuing to follow the Schuller prescription for church success, publicly declared the "vision" he had for his church. In his very first Saddleback sermon, on March 30, 1980, he used the Schuller concept of presenting his vision in a series of "dream" statements. One of the dreams he declared to the sixty or so people in attendance had to do with the future growth of the church.

> **It is the dream** of welcoming 20,000 members into the fellowship of our church family—loving, learning, laughing, and living in harmony together. [4] (Emphasis in original)

After proclaiming the various "dream" components of his vision, Rick Warren continued to follow Schuller's age-old metaphysical technique—a technique I learned in the New Age—of positively and publicly affirming the success of his "dream" in advance of its happening. Rick Warren declared:

> I stand before you today and state in confident assurance that these dreams will become reality. Why? Because they are inspired by God![5]

And the rest is history. Rick Warren's congregation grew and so did his reputation as someone to emulate in ministry. Today, thousands of pastors and churches have adopted his methods and strategies, and he has sold millions of books.

But while everyone else was seeming to sense the presence of God In almost everything Rick Warren was doing, I kept sensing the presence of Robert Schuller.

More Schuller Material

In reading the many Schuller books I had picked up at used book stores, I was continually reminded of the Schuller influence in Rick Warren's writings. In addition to what has already been cited, there was so much more material that I was finding. And I knew there was probably a great deal more information of which I was not even aware.

I discovered that Rick Warren had already established his pattern of using unattributed Schuller material in his first book, *The Purpose-Driven Church*. For example, he dramatically concluded his best-selling book by challenging readers to make their church "a purpose-driven church." With no footnotes or references of any kind, Rick Warren wrote:

> Accept the challenge of becoming a purpose-driven church! The greatest churches in history are yet to be built.[6]

It turns out that his statement, "The greatest churches in history are yet to be built," was almost a direct quotation from Robert Schuller. In Schuller's 1986 book *Your Church Has A Fantastic Future!*, a pastor is quoted as saying:

> Ten years ago, I heard Dr. Robert Schuller say at his leadership conference, "The greatest churches in the world are yet to be built!"[7]

In his 1967 book *Move Ahead with Possibility Thinking*, Schuller explained that his statement about "the greatest churches" was a direct answer from God on whether or not he should start a church in California.

> It was my moment of decision. It was nearly midnight. Wide awake in the top bunk of the Santa Fe railroad car, I stared out the window. The train was stopped now, high in the Arizona mountains. A full moon fell on the snow-covered pines. Suddenly a deer leaped from behind a tree and bounded off into the moonlit night spraying dry snow-dust in his trail. Then, sparked by George Truett's experience, it came to me: the positive possibility thought,
>
> **"The greatest churches have yet to be organized."**
>
> That did it. By the grace of God I was being given the answer to my five-year-old prayer. Here was my chance to build a great church.[8] (Emphasis in original)

Rick Warren's seemingly original exhortation, at the end of his 1995 book, was really the "positive possibility thought" that had come forty years earlier as an answer to Robert Schuller's prayer in 1955.

Other Similarities in Quotes and Citations

Rick Warren's tendency to quote or cite people who are quoted or cited by Schuller is also very evident throughout *The Purpose-Driven Life.* New age leader Bernie Siegel wasn't the only Schuller figure that Rick Warren used in his book. There were many others.

In his 1991 book, *Life's Not Fair, But God Is Good,* Schuller recounted an anecdote that contained a quote by psychologist William James:

> 'The most important thing in life is living your life for something more important than your life.'[9]

Eleven years later in *The Purpose-Driven Life,* Rick Warren wrote:

> William James said, "The best use of life is to spend it for something that outlasts it."[10]

Historian Thomas Carlyle was someone quoted by Robert Schuller as far back as 1969. Schuller quoted Carlyle in his book *Self-Love* as saying, "Man was made for greatness!"[11] Thirty-three years and many other Schuller references to Carlyle later, Rick Warren headlined a Carlyle quote regarding "purpose" to open Chapter Three of *The Purpose-Driven Life*—the same chapter that uses all the other Schuller material regarding "hope" and "purpose."

Long before Rick Warren wrote *The Purpose-Driven Life,* Robert Schuller had quoted Catholic mystics Brother Lawrence and Henri Nouwen, transcendentalist Henry David Thoreau, and theosophist sympathizer George Bernard Shaw. All of these men are quoted or cited by Rick Warren in *The Purpose-Driven Life.*

England's branch of the Theosophical Society cited George Bernard Shaw's interest in the New Age teachings of Theosophy:

> Some of the most influential people of its day were at-

tracted to Theosophy—playwright Oscar Wilde, poet W.B.
Yeats, author George Bernard Shaw...[12]

Despite Shaw's well-known theosophical leanings, Rick
Warren has had no problem quoting him in regard to
"purpose." Why Rick Warren, without any explanation at
all, has used someone drawn to the occultic and New Age
teachings of Theosophy to emphasize being used for "a
purpose" is a real mystery. Nevertheless, he has written:

> George Bernard Shaw wrote, "This is the true joy of life:
> the being used up for a purpose recognized by yourself as
> a mighty one; being a force of nature..."[13]

And in the Schuller tradition, Rick Warren quoted the
former mystic and New Age pioneer Aldous Huxley. After
incorrectly diagnosing the Apostle Paul as suffering from
"doubt" and "depression" rather than persecution, Rick
Warren emphasized the importance of "shared experiences"
by quoting Huxley:

> If Paul had kept his experience of doubt and depression a
> secret, millions of people would never have benefited from
> it. Only shared experiences can help others. Aldous Huxley
> said, "Experience is not what happens to you. It is what
> you do with what happens to you."[14]

Huxley is the single most quoted figure in Marilyn
Ferguson's best-selling New Age book, *The Aquarian Conspiracy*. In relation to "shared experiences" that come from
taking psychedelic drugs, Huxley is quoted as saying:

> "Although these new mind-changers may start by being
> something of an embarrassment, they will tend in the long
> run to deepen the spiritual life of the communities...."[15]
> (Ellipsis dots in original)

Ferguson added:

> Huxley believed that the long-predicted religious revival in the United States would start with drugs, not evangelists.[16]

Rick Warren's citing of the metaphysical Huxley in discussing the importance of "shared experiences" seemed as inappropriate as his referencing New Age leader Bernie Siegel in introducing "hope" and "purpose." Randomly quoting influential New Age figures with no introduction or explanation as to who these people are is not exactly what you expect from a shepherd who is supposed to be protecting his flock.

In addition to the many Schuller people that Rick Warren quotes or cites, there are so many other Schuller references within the pages of *The Purpose-Driven Life*. Many of Rick Warren's words, phrases, ideas, and expressions can be traced back to Schuller. Schuller's use of multiple Bible versions, and even his penchant for instructional rhymes, is imitated. Rick Warren's Schulleresque "God is real, no matter how I feel,"[17] "You are never persuasive when you're abrasive,"[18] and "Revealing your feeling is the beginning of healing"[19] were obviously inspired by Schuller rhymes like: "It takes guts to leave the ruts,"[20] "I'm not free until I believe in me!"[21] and "[I]nch by inch, anything's a cinch."[22] Rick Warren's rhymes were just further reminders of Schuller's pervasive influence in *The Purpose-Driven Life*.

More Examples of Schuller Material

In his 1997 book, *If It's Going to Be, It's Up to Me: The Eight Proven Principles of Possibility Thinking*, Robert Schuller included an extended section on the importance of listening to your heart. In this section entitled "Start with the heart," he wrote:

Connect with this cosmic Higher Power. Listen to the call
of your heart of hearts to become a believer in God.[23]

Listen to me! Listen to me—I'm your heart. Why do you
never dare to let me be free to become what I was born to
become? Your passionate power.[24]

Listen to me, my honored one, for God lives within your
heart.[25]

Connect with me and come to love and listen to the God
within you.[26]

Rick Warren included a similar section in *The Purpose-Driven Life* entitled "Listening To Your Heart." He stated that when you connect with your heart you are connecting with the "real you." He explained that the heart is "the bundle of desires, hopes, interests, ambitions, dreams, and affections you have." He said another word for the heart is "passion."

Rick Warren, in the "Listening To Your Heart" section of his 2002 book, wrote:

Another word for heart is *passion*.[27]

God wants you to serve him passionately...[28]

Passion drives perfection.[29]

Schuller, in the "Start with the heart" section of his 1997 book, wrote:

Passion is the key to success. Every achiever I've met is quick to admit that the passion for his or her dream made it happen.[30]

Given that Rick Warren is believing a Bible version that says that God is "in" and within everything, his statements about the heart when blended with Schuller's seem to me to be saying almost the exact same thing:

> I'm your heart.... Listen to your heart.... Connect with me and listen to the God within you.... Your heart is your passion.... Passion drives perfection and is the key to your success.

When I was involved with New Age teachings I was taught the same thing: to "listen to your heart" and to follow the "God within." Years ago, when I "listened to my heart" and "passionately" followed "the God within," I ended up going further and further into New Age teachings. It all *felt* so good. Obviously a passionate heart can be a wonderful source of love and inspiration. But the Bible warns us that it can also be a source of great deception.

> The heart is deceitful above all *things*, and desperately wicked: who can know it? (Jeremiah 17:9)

> For out of the heart proceed evil thoughts, murders, adulteries, fornications, thefts, false witness, blasphemies. (Matthew 15:19)

Curiously, earlier in *The Purpose-Driven Life* Rick Warren had warned about temptation that comes from "within us" and "out of a person's heart."[31] Yet, 34 pages later he urged the reader to listen to their heart because it reveals "the real you." I was to learn that this was not the only time Rick Warren had overridden what seemed to be a warning with a clearly contradictory statement.

Think Globally

In another section in the same 1997 Robert Schuller book, *If It's Going to Be, It's Up to Me*, Schuller described humanity's universal need for hope and self-esteem under the heading, "Think globally; act locally."[32]

In *The Purpose-Driven Life*, Rick Warren also included a section devoted to "thinking globally." Entitling this section "Shift from local thinking to global thinking,"[33] he stressed the importance of shifting our thinking to the global level. He urged "world-class Christians" to pray for the world and then "dared" them to get involved. He said, "I dare you to dive into the deep end."[34]

"Daring" someone to take action is the prescribed "third step" of Robert Schuller's "Mountain-Moving Faith" formula.[35] In his 1967 book, *Move Ahead with Possibility Thinking*, Schuller wrote:

> Mountain-moving faith is faith that dares to step into deep water.[36]

Thirty-five years later, Rick Warren has not only used Schuller's "dare" principle, he has also used Schuller's metaphor of water, and even the same word "deep":

> I dare you to dive into the deep end.[37]

Mentally Soaked by Robert Schuller?

I am quite sure that further study would reveal there is much more additional Schuller material contained in the pages of *The Purpose-Driven Life*. I certainly had not gone out looking for all of this. I just kept discovering these things as I read along and followed up on what I was reading. I had no idea going into my reading of *The Purpose-Driven Life* how thoroughly the presence of Robert Schuller inhabits its pages. Because Robert Schuller's name is never even mentioned in *The Purpose-Driven Life*, most readers would never know how much of Rick Warren's material is actually drawn from the writings and teachings of Robert Schuller. They would never know how inextricably intertwined the two men's teachings seem to be.

In his book *You Can Become The Person You Want To Be,* Schuller described one of the purposes of his Institute:

> In the Institute for Successful Church Leadership, which I conduct in Garden Grove, California, we aim to turn ministers and church leaders into dynamic Positive Thinkers.[38]

In his 1995 book, *Prayer: My Soul's Adventure With God,* Schuller described the effect he had on a young Irish pastor that had come to his Institute:

> "But he had been mentally soaked with Possibility Thinking by this American preacher."[39]

Rick Warren certainly seems to be another example of a pastor who has been "mentally soaked" by Schuller's teachings. Schuller has obviously had a "profound" influence on Rick Warren. Most people will probably never know *how* profound.

As a self-proclaimed "change agent,"[40] it seemed that one of Rick Warren's unstated purposes was to mainstream Robert Schuller's teachings into the more traditional "Bible-based" wing of the Church. Many believers who seem to trust Rick Warren, ironically, do not trust Robert Schuller. Rick Warren's "magic" seems to be able to make the teachings of Robert Schuller palatable to believers who would have otherwise never accepted these same teachings had they come directly from Schuller himself. And, as I was about to discover, one of Rick Warren's colleagues was also in the process of doing much the same thing.

Chapter 11

God's Dream?

I had this Big Dream...[1]

Robert Schuller
Reach Out for New Life, 1977

We really are somebodies![2]

Robert Schuller
Self-Esteem: The New Reformation, 1982

**"The Dream Giver gave me a Big Dream!
I was made to be a Somebody..."**[3]

Bruce Wilkinson
The Dream Giver, 2003

In the midst of reading Rick Warren and Robert Schuller, I noticed that Bruce Wilkinson, author of *The Prayer of Jabez*, had a new book entitled *The Dream Giver*. I bought it and read it the next day. When I read it, I felt like I was reading yet another book by Robert Schuller. The entire book was about encouraging people to pursue and achieve the "Big Dream" that Wilkinson claims God, the "Dream Giver," has put in everyone's heart. In the preface, Wilkinson wrote:

> I have yet to find a person who *didn't* have a dream. They may not be able to describe it. They may have forgotten it. They may no longer believe in it.
>
> But it's there.
>
> I call this universal and powerful longing a Big Dream.[4]

Like Rick Warren, Wilkinson makes no mention of Robert Schuller anywhere in his book, yet he uses Schuller's teachings on achieving one's dreams to frame and underline almost everything that he presents about dreams. Wilkinson's seemingly original use of the term "Big Dream," with a capital "B" and a capital "D," was used by Schuller at least as far back as 1977. Many other references, subtle and not so subtle, can be directly attributed to dream material found in Schuller's writings and teachings over the last four decades. As a matter of fact, "Dreaming" is the first step of Robert Schuller's formulaic "Eight Steps of Mountain-Moving Faith."[5]

Achieving the Big Dream

Wilkinson's book *The Dream Giver* is a parable about a man named "Ordinary" pursuing his "Big Dream" to become a "Somebody." Ordinary is used to introduce the Schuller concept that man's "destiny" is to become a "Somebody" and to achieve "Greatness." Ordinary exclaims:

> "The Dream Giver gave me a Big Dream! I was made to be a Somebody and destined to achieve Great Things!"[6]

Ordinary then leaves the land of the "Familiar" and heads toward "the Border." And as he does, Wilkinson introduces the "dare" language that is part of Robert Schuller's "Mountain-Moving Faith" formula.

> He was heading toward the Border, where almost no Nobodies ever went.
>
> Ordinary had never dared to walk this way before.[7]

But as he reaches the "Borderland," he experiences fear of the unknown and he doubts his Dream. When he starts to lose faith, he is encouraged by "the Dream Giver."

> "I'm not the right Nobody to go after such a Big Dream."
>
> *Yes, you are*, said the Dream Giver. *I made you to do this.*
>
> "But I don't think I *can* do this," he said.
>
> *Yes, you can. And I will be with you. I will help you.*[8]

Then "Border Bullies," those people who oppose his Dream, try to keep him from achieving his Dream by driving him back into the land of the "Familiar." His family blocks his view of the "bridge" that leads to his "Big Dream." His uncle tells him that in his attempt to cross "the Border" he is going against their "every tradition." But Ordinary is helped by people who are sympathetic and want him to achieve his Dream. These are the "Border Busters" who help him cross "the Border" so he can move on towards his Dream.

But once he gets across "the Border" he finds himself in a "Wasteland." After several trying days in the Wasteland, Ordinary doubts his Dream and the Dream Giver. But when all seems hopeless, he awakes one morning to suddenly find himself in "Sanctuary" and in the presence of the Dream Giver. At this point, the Dream Giver asks Ordinary to surrender his Dream. So Ordinary gives his Dream back to the Dream Giver, who is described as the one who had actually given him his Dream in the first place. The Dream Giver proceeds to bless Ordinary's Dream and then returns his Dream back to him. It is now *their* Dream. What had previously been just Ordinary's own personal Dream was now part of the Dream Giver's "Big Dream" for the world.

> Now when Ordinary looked at his surrendered Dream, he saw that it had grown. Now his Dream was no longer only about Ordinary. Now it was part of the Dream Giver's Big

Dream for the whole world.[9]

But even with the Dream Giver's blessing of what is now *their* Dream, Ordinary continues to be tested. In the "Valley of the Giants," he encounters new opposition to his Dream from what seem to be insurmountable "Giants." But in the midst of his trials, he is encouraged by other "Dreamers" like himself that he meets along the way and who share his Dream. Ultimately, Ordinary, with help from the Dream Giver, meets and defeats the "Giant of Darkness" and in so doing brings honor and glory to the Dream Giver.

> Every Giant was another opportunity for the Dream Giver to receive honor.[10]

With the Dream Giver's help, Ordinary achieves his Big Dream. But soon, Ordinary—who has now become a "Somebody"—understands that the Dream Giver's Big Dream will continue to evolve. It will now grow into "a new and even bigger Dream."

> He was ready now for the Dream to grow into a new and bigger Dream.[11]

The "Dream Coach"

*I*n the second half of the book, Wilkinson presents himself as the "Dream Coach." He assures the reader that his counsel comes from "years of experience as a Dreamer." Continuing to draw deeply from Schuller's teachings about Dreams—but still without citing Schuller—Wilkinson encourages the reader to learn the lessons that Ordinary had learned in the parable: the importance of "waking up" to your "Big Dream," then setting out to achieve it, and the importance of understanding that you are "destined" to be a "Somebody" and "to achieve Great Things."

But the truth Ordinary discovered from the Dream Giver is that every Nobody was made to be a Somebody. And the key to discovering all you are meant to do and be is to wake up to the Big Dream God has given you and set out on a journey to achieve it.[12]

The Big Dream told him that he, a Nobody, was made to be a Somebody and destined to achieve Great Things.[13]

Wilkinson reminds the reader that each person is an indispensable part of God's "Big Dream" to meet the world's needs:

You have been handcrafted by God to accomplish a part of His Big Dream for the world. How? Your Big Dream is meant to fulfill a Big Need he cares deeply about. The reason you're here is to take a part of His Dream from Point A to Point B. No one else can do it quite like you.[14]

Wilkinson encourages the reader to push on past his or her fears and past the various adversarial people—the "Border Bullies"—who try to keep them from achieving their Dream.

You know you're ready to move past your Border Bullies when you realize that their objections belong to Familiar. But you don't live there anymore.

The Border is the furthest edge of your old life. One more step and you will walk into your new one.[15]

Wilkinson says, from his own experience in "the Borderland," that "the larger the vision" the more opposition there will be from the "Border Bullies." But he encourages the reader to push on beyond the "Border" of the "Familiar" into a new and "wonderful future."

> Make your crossing, Dreamer. Your wonderful future is
> waiting. And the Dream Giver is ready to help you find it.[16]

He warns readers that even with an understanding of the Dream they will still encounter doubts and fears that will test their Dream. But he reminds them from the parable that the testing is just part of their preparation for the ultimate achievement of their Dream—the Dream that is actually their unique part of God's Dream.

Describing the Dreamer's final plunge into the unknown as a test of faith, and comparing it to the Israelites going through the Wilderness on the way to the promised land, Wilkinson suggests this prayer:

> "Please make me into the person I need to be to do the
> Dream You have created me to do!"[17]

Wilkinson concludes his book with words reminiscent of Robert Schuller and Rick Warren's previously cited references to Thomas Carlyle—that man's "purpose" is to realize he was "made for greatness." He urges the reader to go for the "greatness" that will come from pursuing the "Big Dream" that God has put in their heart.

> Greatness is your real future. Are you ready for the wonder
> of it?[18]

Three days after I finished reading *The Dream Giver*, Bruce Wilkinson appeared on Robert Schuller's *Hour of Power* television program. Preaching from Schuller's pulpit at the Crystal Cathedral and sounding much like Schuller himself, Wilkinson spoke about the importance of realizing one's dreams.

Bruce Wilkinson on the Hour of Power

On October 26, 2003, Robert Schuller's son welcomed guest pastor Bruce Wilkinson to the Crystal Cathedral and to their worldwide telecast of the *Hour of Power*:

> What a wonderful day to be in God's presence here. You are going to hear words this morning that will change your life. It's a powerful morning....
>
> You'll want to listen very attentively because what he [Wilkinson] has to say is profound.[19]

Although he never mentioned Robert Schuller in his book, Bruce Wilkinson began his talk by finally acknowledging Schuller's huge influence in the area of "living your dream,"

> Good morning, everyone. I want to talk about dreams. Of all places in the world to talk about dreams this is the place...because I think Dr. Schuller is the patriarch, in the work about living your dream.[20] (Ellipsis dots in original)

Then Wilkinson defined what he meant by "dream."

> I want to talk to you about your dream today, that part of your heart that if you think about it, you become emotional. It's that dream that you wish..."if I had all the money in all the world and I could do whatever I wanted to do, that's what I would love to do." That's called **your dream**.[21] (Emphasis and ellipsis dots in original)

Wilkinson then proceeded to challenge everyone to go for their "Big Dream." It was the same message that was in his book *The Dream Giver*—you have a "Dream" in your heart, and God will help you achieve your Dream because it is your unique part of the "Big Dream" that God has for the world. Wilkinson told everyone not to focus on their fears but on their Dream:

> Fulfilling God's dream is what you have been made to do,
> therefore, what do you do? You don't wait for the fear to
> leave. You breakthrough your fear. It's the will of God that
> we follow the dream. If you don't follow your dream, do
> you realize how many people will be affected because you
> didn't follow your dream? You see, **a dream is helping
> somebody else's dream**. It is God's dream and **God's
> dream is never selfish**....You can't imagine the more you
> pursue the dream, the more God is going to use you in
> ways you never imagined possible.[22] (Emphasis in original)

He concluded by stating that if everyone follows the
Dream that God has *purposefully* placed in their hearts, they
will "change the world."

> I want to pray for you because you are the people who are
> going to change the world. What a touching moment it is
> to you and me and heaven above when men and women
> respond to the call of God to follow the dream that He has
> placed in their hearts to say "no" to fear anymore...or "I
> can't"...or "I won't" anymore, but to say, "Lord God,
> please let me do the dream. Please let me do the dream."[23]

He then prayed:

> Our Father in Heaven, this church, this staff, this team has
> stood for following the dream for decades. And I have been
> the recipient many, many times from the messages from
> this pulpit from both father and son. I thank You that they
> have encouraged me all these years to follow the dream.
> And now I stand by their side proclaiming the truth of
> God's word once again.[24]

Bruce Wilkinson at Saddleback Church

The same day that Bruce Wilkinson was televised on

Robert Schuller's *Hour of Power*, he also spoke at Rick Warren's Saddleback Church.[25] Rick Warren introduced him as "one of my best friends in the whole world" and enthusiastically described Wilkinson's new book, *The Dream Giver*, as an "unbelievable book." He said that Wilkinson's talk would be "based out of the principles out of the Bible that are taught in this book."

Wilkinson told the Saddleback congregation and his Internet audience that everyone has a "personal Dream." He stated that the whole area of one's "personal Dream" was something that "needs to be resurrected across the world." He said that "people need to know their Dream" and people need to "live their Dream." He said that "everyone has a Dream" in their heart and that this Dream is their "destiny." He told them the reason they have this Dream is because God has put this Dream in their heart.

He told everyone that they should "find out what their Dream is." Wilkinson emphasized, as he did at the Crystal Cathedral, that each person's Dream is connected to everyone else's dream because it is really "God's Dream." He warned that when people don't "do" their "Dream" it can negatively impact everyone else's Dream for "generations" afterwards. Each person must look to the Dream that is in their heart, see it as "God's Dream," submit the Dream to God and then "commit to that Dream." He said that if the Dream is in your heart it is "probably" what God wants you to do. *Where is this found in the Bible?*

Wilkinson commended everyone at Saddleback for their ability to achieve Dreams, and then he told them that Saddleback Church is in "the midst of an historic moment."

> The platform that God has given to Saddleback Church in Orange County is large. But whether or not you know this or not, the platform that God is giving to this church is far larger in the world than it is here. And you are at an

historic moment because you are at the front of the wedge
of the Spirit of Almighty God. And what Pastor Rick is
going to share next week about the Saddleback global
vision is right from heaven's heart. I promise. I know what
it is. It's like that. And I want you to understand something. I've never said this to any other church and I never
would 'cause it's the only church I believe it's true of.
History is being made here.... *World Religion*

And I'm here to say to you as a fellow believer, you must
rise up. You must fulfill the destiny that God has for this
church. 'Cause I want to say something to you—it will
revolutionize the world. And that is not an overstatement.
Will you therefore open your heart? Will you prepare for
the Dream that's coming?

Later he prayed:

Father in heaven, how we love to live in history. History's
being made right now....

We ask you, Holy Spirit, that your full and complete Dream
for this church and every person in this audience, that this
will be the greatest living illustration in the history of the
church. About what one group of people who sense their
destiny, can rise to the occasion and that the world is
radically transformed. We are honored, Lord, by your
presence. In Jesus' name. Amen.

God's Dream for Our Self-Esteem?

When Bruce Wilkinson ended his prayer by saying, "in
Jesus' name," I realized that it was the first time Jesus'
name had been mentioned in his whole talk about dreams.
It had been the same thing at the Crystal Cathedral. Nor
could Jesus' name be found anywhere in Wilkinson's book
The Dream Giver. Maybe it was because Jesus never talked
about "living your dreams." When the Bible says that in the
last days "your old men shall dream dreams" it isn't talking

about these kinds of dreams. The only dreams mentioned in the Bible are dreams that occur during sleep. Biblical dreams and visions have *nothing* to do with those that are imagined and found in men's hearts—the kind of "dreams" Wilkinson was describing. The dream process Wilkinson was suggesting had nothing to do with the teachings of the Bible, but it had everything to do with the teachings of Robert Schuller.

Rick Warren had stated that Wilkinson's talk would be "based out of the principles of the Bible that are taught in this book." But Wilkinson hadn't discussed any biblical principles because there are no biblical principles about *this* kind of dreaming. The term "God's Dream" cannot be found in the Bible. But it is a term that I would later discover Robert Schuller has been using for many years. In his 1982 book, *Self-Esteem: The New Reformation,* Robert Schuller wrote:

"...And follow me"? What does that mean? It means daring to dream a great dream![26] (Ellipsis dots in original)

I am not fully forgiven until I allow God to write his new dream for my life on the blackboard of my mind, and I dare to believe "I am; therefore, I can. I am a child of God. I am somebody. God has a great plan to redeem society. He needs me and wants to use me."[27]

"God's forgiving grace is incomplete until he gives me—and I accept—a new kingdom-building dream and opportunity."[28]

I must accept the dream God gives me and develop its inherent possibilities.[29]

When God's dream is accepted, we must be prepared to pay a high price....But the path will lead us through the valley of potential humiliation before the **crown of godly pride** is placed upon our heads.[30] (Emphasis added;

contrast this with Isaiah 28:1-5)

> **The cross Christ calls us to bear will be offered as a dream**, an idea. It is not imposed; we must *choose* to fully accept it. It will appear as an inspiring idea that would incarnate itself in a form of ministry that helps self-esteem-impoverished persons to discover their self-worth through salvation and subsequent social service in our Savior's name.[31] (Emphasis added; italics in original)

> Tremendous human energy is needed to walk God's walk, work God's work, fulfill God's will, and **complete his dream for our self-esteem**.[32] (Emphasis added)

Man of the Hour

Rick Warren was getting most of the publicity, but it seemed that Robert Schuller was really the man of the hour. Christian leaders Rick Warren and Bruce Wilkinson both had best-selling books that depended heavily on Schuller material. Neale Donald Walsch and his New Age "God" were praising Schuller and quoting from his book *Self-Esteem: The New Reformation*. And even evangelicals were officially recognizing Schuller as one of their own. Four months after Robert Schuller emphatically declared, "Yes, God is alive and He is in every single human being!" he was a featured speaker at the 2004 annual convention of the National Association of Evangelicals. He took the occasion to call for a "new reformation" and to tell everyone gathered that he thought *Self-Esteem: The New Reformation* was the best book that he had ever written.[33]

Things were moving so fast. Everything spiritual was being presented in such "positive" Schulleresque terms: God's "Purpose," God's "Dream," God's "Destiny," God "in" everyone and "in" everything. There were almost no warnings about possible deception, nor any calls for spiritual discernment. The only warnings were about the "Border

Bullies" who might interfere with their "mission" by questioning what they were doing. The "Border Bullies" who would try to keep "Ordinary" from becoming a "Somebody," by keeping him stuck in the "old" and away from the "new."

But was anyone testing the spirits? Wilkinson's parable seemed to neatly parallel the "Jabez temptation" to "enlarge" one's faith by accepting the principles of the New Spirituality. Was Bruce Wilkinson aware of how his two books could be used to falsely encourage believers to let go of "familiar" Christian doctrine by being "daring" enough to "enlarge" the "borders" of what they believe? Was he, or anyone else, seeing that maybe there was another hand in all of this?

Interestingly, Wayne Dyer and other New Age leaders were also using the term "God's Dream" and referring to this dream process to push the idea of Oneness. In his book *You'll See It When You Believe It*, and in the chapter entitled "Oneness," Dyer wrote:

> Who is the ultimate dreamer? Call it as you will: God, higher consciousness, Krishna, spirit, whatever pleases you....
>
> One dream, one dreamer, billions of embodied characters acting out that one dream...Your true essence is that you are part and parcel of the one big dream.[34]
>
> This is the quintessential message that is available from all of the spiritual masters. The way to glimpse it is through the mystical world that you are able to create for yourself and live out in your dreaming body. You, the dreamer... God, the dreamer.[35] (Ellipsis dots in original)
>
> I assure you that when you truly know that there is only one dream and that you are connected to everyone in that dream, you begin to think and act as if you are connected to it all, rather than attached to your separateness.[36]

At the time of Wilkinson's appearance at the Crystal Cathedral and at Saddleback Church, I had been reading Robert Schuller's 2001 autobiography, *My Journey: From an Iowa Farm to a Cathedral of Dreams.* Toward the end of the book Schuller had written:

> As the century, as well as the millennium, drew to a close, I was astounded to see how much my perspective had shifted. In my early years my world was Sioux County, Iowa, and the Dutch Reformed Church, but now I had a global awareness. Going "somewhere" from "nowhere" had begun to take on a whole new meaning. **I was moving further and further into a mindset of religious inclusivity.** This was another "edge," to be sure—but I had by now grown comfortable living on that edge. In fact, I liked it![37] (Emphasis added)

And then, almost at the very end of his book, he described the "bold impossible dream" that he was dreaming for the world.

> And I'm dreaming a bold impossible dream: that positive thinking believers in God will rise above the illusions that our sectarian religions have imposed on the world, and that leaders of the major faiths will rise above doctrinal idiosyncrasies, choosing not to focus on disagreements, but rather to **transcend** divisive dogmas to work together to bring peace and prosperity and hope to the world.[38] (Emphasis added)

Certainly the idea of peace is one that resounds in the hearts of all mankind. But, as I looked at Schuller's words, one word stuck out above them all. It was the word "transcend." Schuller was using *the very same word* that Neale Donald Walsch's New Age "God" had used to answer Walsch's question about how "to get past" all of the different "mixed-up" spiritual beliefs that prevent world peace. "God" had told Walsch:

> There is a way....
>
> **Transcend** them....
>
> Transcending means to go beyond, to move past....
>
> "Transcending" does not mean always being "other than,"
> it means always being "larger than." Your new, larger belief
> system will no doubt retain some of the old—that part of
> the old belief system that you experience as still serving
> you—and so it will be a combination of the new and the
> old, not a rejection of the old from top to bottom.[39]
> (Emphasis added)

Robert Schuller has a "bold impossible dream" that
people of all faiths will move past "doctrinal idiosyncracies"
and "transcend divisive dogmas" so that they can attain
"God's Dream" for world peace. Neale Donald Walsch and
his New Age "God" are proposing a 5-Step PEACE Plan that
will "transcend" these differences. It is a 5-Step PEACE Plan
they claim will bring global peace if the world will adopt the
principles of their New Spirituality. A PEACE Plan that
seems to fit the description of Robert Schuller's "bold
impossible dream." A PEACE Plan that Walsch and his New
Age "God" might even describe as "God's Dream for the
world."

Chapter 12

Rick Warren's
P.E.A.C.E. Plan

Is this new venture why you were born?
Is this daring dream God's purpose for your life?[1]
Robert Schuller
If It's Going to Be, It's Up to Me, 1997

A friend had left Rick Warren's e-mail at my door. It was dated October 27, 2003, one day after Bruce Wilkinson had spoken about dreams at Saddleback Church. Using the exact phrase "God's Dream" that Wilkinson had discussed at Saddleback the day before and that Robert Schuller had introduced at least 25 years before that, Rick Warren titled this e-mail "GOD'S DREAM FOR YOU—AND THE WORLD." In it he announced that he would be introducing what he was calling his "Global P.E.A.C.E. plan" that upcoming weekend.

In a series of enthusiastic and authoritative statements, Rick Warren was positively declaring that the Purpose-Driven Church had arrived at its "moment of destiny." He affirmed that God was preparing their church for "a great dream to change the world." He said that the dream that they were about to embark upon would "change history." Employing a metaphysical dream affirmation technique (now often called "vision casting") and using precise Schuller language, he declared that "The Global Peace Plan IS GOING TO HAPPEN." Rick Warren's e-mail read, in part:

This past weekend there was so much enthusiasm..
energy.. and expectation in our church. You could sense
that God is preparing our church for a great dream to
change the world! *For Satan & the Antichrist*

Bruce Wilkinson reaffirmed that fact in his powerful
message on God's dream for your life. The stages of a
dream fulfillment for each of us as individuals also applies
to us together as a church family....

THIS WEEKEND, I'll begin a series of five messages on
God's dream to use you globally - to literally use YOU to
help change the world! I'll unveil our Global P.E.A.C.E.
plan, and how God has uniquely prepared you for this
moment of destiny.

You are not a part of Saddleback Church by accident. God
has brought all of us together, at this very strategic
moment in time, to make a difference. I say this without
fear of exaggeration - God is going to use you, and all of us
together at Saddleback, to change history! *World Order & Religion*

Only one other time in my life have I felt this deep conviction - and was the day God called me at age 25 to begin
Saddleback Church with no money and no members. *Yes to work for The Antich...*

The Global Peace Plan IS GOING TO HAPPEN - and I know
that God has brought you specifically to our church family
at this time because he wants to use you in some way.[2]

I sat in my room reading and re-reading Rick Warren's
e-mail. Things were moving very fast in this Purpose-Driven
movement. The Robert Schuller influence, already so
obvious in Rick Warren's writings, was becoming even more
apparent as Bruce Wilkinson and Rick Warren were now
introducing Schuller's teachings on dreams into the Church.
Teachings on dreams that were based on man's word rather
than God's Word.

Instead of contending for the faith by exposing the
plans of our spiritual Adversary's 5-Step PEACE Plan, Rick
Warren was in the process of introducing his own 5-Step

P.E.A.C.E. Plan—a P.E.A.C.E. Plan that was being presented in the name of God and in the form of a dream. A dream that was being described in Schuller dream language as "God's Dream for the world."

The P.E.A.C.E. Plan Unveiled

That next week on November 2, 2003, Rick Warren unveiled his 5-Step P.E.A.C.E. Plan to Saddleback Church and to everyone watching on the Internet.[3] He began his exhortation by telling everyone that it was an "historic day" as they were "beginning a new phase in the history of Saddleback Church." He recounted that he and his wife started Saddleback in January of 1980 when he was only twenty-five years old, and that they had made a "40 year commitment" to the Church and to the community. He said the first ten years of ministry were ones of "local blessing." He said that in the decade of the nineties they went "national," as they wanted "to help churches around the nation." He described how they taught seminars and provided resources and training to assist over 250,000 churches across America.

He said that now that it was the twenty-first century, they were "going global." They weren't going to stop their work locally or nationally, but now it was time "to bless the whole world." Using language straight out of Bruce Wilkinson's book *The Dream Giver*, Rick Warren said that God is most glorified when you go after "the biggest Giants." His wife, Kay, then described these "Giants" as spiritual lostness, the lack of servant leadership, poverty, disease, and ignorance. Later, Rick Warren said that the forces in his church, and in churches around the world, would be mobilized to take on these "Giant" problems that afflicted billions of people around the world. He said the church was uniquely equipped and the only world resource that could realistically deal with these "Global Giants." He said that the problems weren't new, but that his P.E.A.C.E. Plan methodology of confronting these "Giants" would be "revolutionary."

Rick Warren said that Saddleback would be formulating a plan that would eventually be shared with "millions of other churches." He stated that together "we are going to change the world." He reminded everyone that there are 72,000 names on the Saddleback Church roll and how that number of people was like "a city." He said he was as sure about the success of this plan as he was when he started Saddleback twenty-three years ago. He told everyone that they were not at Saddleback "by accident" and that God wanted to use everyone to accomplish the P.E.A.C.E. Plan.

He said that sometimes it is necessary "to go to the next level of spiritual growth." He remarked that they had been "blessed" at Saddleback to have "great teachers like Bruce Wilkinson." He stated that those who have been so blessed must be a blessing to others. Christians must reach out to others.

In the same way that Neale Donald Walsch used the word "peace" as an acronym for presenting his 5-Step PEACE Plan, Rick Warren also used the word "peace" as an acronym for presenting his 5-Step P.E.A.C.E. Plan:

Rick Warren's 5-Step P.E.A.C.E. Plan

P lant Churches

E quip Leaders

A ssist the Poor

C are for the Sick

E ducate the Next Generation[4]

"I Don't Understand It All, But Count Me In."

In this same sermon, Rick Warren positively affirmed "we're going to make history" and echoed Robert Schuller's call for a "new reformation." He stated that, as churches were re-formed and people were mobilized, there was no reason that the Great Commission of taking the Gospel to the world couldn't be fulfilled "in this generation."

He quoted 2 Corinthians 5:18-19 from a new Bible version that substituted the single word "peace" for the commonly translated words "reconcile," "reconciled," and "reconciliation."

> God sent Christ to make peace between himself and us. And he's given us the work of making peace between himself and others. God was in Christ offering peace and forgiveness to the people of this world. And now he has given us the work of sharing his message about peace. (CEV)

Rick Warren drew special attention to the repeated use of the word "peace" in this Bible verse but did not mention that the word "peace" only appears in the newer Bible versions. He said, "And notice all of the times the word 'peace' is used in this passage." Then, describing the Church as "the real peace corps," he said:

> It is our job, it is our responsibility, to help people make peace with God and then to help them make peace with each other. That is the commission that was given not to a government, but to the Church.

He said that he had been thinking and praying about all of this over the last year. Rick Warren also said he had been talking to world leaders and getting their opinions, too, and that this 5-Step P.E.A.C.E. Plan was what he came up with.

He said that as it was developed and perfected, it would be shared with churches around the world, just as they had done with the teachings and principles of the Purpose-Driven Church.

Clearly implying that God wants to use the Purpose-Driven P.E.A.C.E. Plan to provide a foundation for world peace and that this effort could hasten the return of Jesus through the fulfillment of the Great Commission, Rick Warren declared:

> You know what God is doing? He is preparing the distribution channel. God is preparing a platform to do peace.

He added:

> God blesses those who work for peace. For they will be called the children of God.

Concluding, he urged everyone to pray about how they could be used in the P.E.A.C.E. Plan.

> Now you pray, say God, I don't understand it all. I don't know why or when or how or where, but I'm saying to you, use me. I'm saying the two most dangerous words in life, Lord—use me—and I don't understand it all, but count me in.

Something Is Not Right

As I reflected on Rick Warren's P.E.A.C.E. Plan, there was no denying that, in theory, it was a very noble and worthwhile undertaking that he was proposing. Sharing the Gospel with those who are spiritually lost, while helping those who are sick, poor and hurting, is what Jesus is all about. One might wonder what could possibly be wrong with reaching out to the world in this way? I had little doubt that Rick Warren would probably mobilize millions of people and accomplish some wonderful things. But over the last month or so as I read *The Purpose-Driven Life*, and now as I was listening to him talk about "God's Dream" for the world and God's "P.E.A.C.E. Plan" for the world, I was deeply troubled. He was sounding not only like Robert Schuller, but more and more like Neale Donald Walsch.

Rick Warren, claiming to be inspired by God, has presented a 5-Step P.E.A.C.E. Plan that he authoritatively declares to be God's plan to "change history." Neale Donald Walsch, claiming to be inspired by "God," also has presented a 5-Step PEACE Plan that he says is God's plan to "change the course of history." Walsch wrote:

> The universe does nothing **by accident**....
>
> You can **change the course of human history**.
>
> This is not an **exaggeration**.[5] (Emphasis added)

Rick Warren stated:

> You are not a part of Saddleback Church **by accident**....I say this without fear of **exaggeration**—God is going to use you, and all of us together at Saddleback, to **change history**![6] (Emphasis added)

But something was clearly amiss. Why would God "do peace" by inspiring a Christian leader to use a similar 5-Step P.E.A.C.E. Plan format as that of a New Age leader whose 5-Step PEACE Plan is totally antagonistic to the Bible's true Gospel of Jesus Christ? The God of the Bible is not a God of confusion (1 Corinthians 14:33). And He does not want his people to be ignorant of the Adversary's schemes (2 Corinthians 2:11). He would want the 5-Step PEACE Plan of the New Spirituality exposed and brought into the light (Ephesians 5:11-13), not confusedly imitated.

It was also very troubling that Rick Warren was continuing to use the teachings of Robert Schuller to drive and motivate his Purpose-Driven Church. Having already discovered Rick Warren's use of unattributed Schuller material in *The Purpose-Driven Life*, I noted that he was now using Schuller's teachings on dreams—reintroduced through Bruce Wilkinson's book—to provide the inspirational foundation for his 5-Step P.E.A.C.E. Plan. And now he was even using the Schuller term "God's Dream" to describe this P.E.A.C.E. Plan. I would later find that Rick Warren's use of the term "God's Dream" and his accompanying affirmation that it is "going to happen" could be found in Schuller's writings as far back as 1978. In *Discover Your Possibilities*, Schuller had written:

> Pray, seek God's guidance and what's going to happen? You'll get a dream to pursue....Find a dream. Once you've got that dream and you know it's **God's dream** for your life, then be daring. Dare to say it. Let the redeemed of the Lord say so. Announce to the whole world that **it's going to happen**.[7] (Emphasis added)

In Rick Warren's October 27, 2003 e-mail entitled "God's Dream For You—And The World," he wrote:

> THIS WEEKEND, I'll begin a series of five messages on **God's dream** to use you globally—to literally use YOU to change the world! I'll unveil our Global P.E.A.C.E. plan, and how God has uniquely prepared you for this moment of destiny....
>
> The Global Peace Plan **IS GOING TO HAPPEN**...[8]
> (Emphasis added; caps in original)

Was the Church *really* going to be able to help defeat the first "Giant" of "spiritual lostness," as it moved more and more deeply into the teachings of Robert Schuller—

teachings that were constantly evolving, and that were sounding more and more like the New Spirituality? So much of what I had discovered in *The Purpose-Driven Life* had its origins in Robert Schuller and mystical New Age thought. Yet Rick Warren seemed, at least on the surface, to be totally oblivious to the New Age implications of what Schuller and he were teaching.

Scripture describes how "peace" will be the way the Antichrist "wonderfully" deceives the world (Daniel 8:23-25, KJB). Christians need to beware of being deceived into aiding and abetting the plans of this coming world ruler.

Small Groups for a False Peace

In my 2002 book, *Reinventing Jesus Christ*, I described how New Age leaders were all over the media after the events of September 11th, 2001. Having formed a single unified organization entitled The Global Renaissance Alliance, these New Age leaders were urging people to gather together in small groups to envision and pray for world peace. A frightened world was told by Neale Donald Walsch, Marianne Williamson, Wayne Dyer, and other New Age leaders that the collective *dream* of world peace could be created if *small groups* around the world focused their prayers, meditations, and visualizations on the single subject of world peace.

Global Renaissance Alliance co-founder Marianne Williamson presented her carefully cloaked New Age ideas on *The Oprah Winfrey Show* shortly after September 11th. Referring to the tragic events of September 11th, Williamson suggested a peace plan based on New Age principles. She introduced a plan that she and other New Age leaders were describing as "the alternative to Armageddon" and that Neale Donald Walsch's New Age "God" would soon be presenting as his 5-Step PEACE Plan. Williamson told

Oprah's millions of viewers that small groups could change the world. She stated:

> Every problem comes bearing its own solution....I think this tragedy has taken us to a ground of being that is like a precious vial of spiritual medicine.
>
> ...So I think now we shouldn't underestimate how much good can come from just talking among ourselves, and atoning. You know, a nation atones, and I think...people around the world can feel us.
>
> ...I've been very involved with people sitting in **small groups**, praying, meditating and speaking from our hearts about what really matters. You know, the terrorists have cells. We hear about the terrorist cells. Well, we need **cells of peace**.[9] (Emphasis added)

When Williamson told Oprah's viewers that humanity needed to "atone," she didn't explain that her definition of atonement was the "at-one-ment" of a New Spirituality. A New Spirituality that promised a world peace based on humanity's shared belief that we are all "at-one" with each other because God is "in" everyone and everything.

Williamson's New Age partner and fellow Global Renaissance Alliance member Wayne Dyer appeared on a post-September 11th PBS special entitled "There's A Spiritual Solution To Every Problem." Also stressing the New Age belief that God is "in" everyone and everything, Dyer suggested that world peace could be realized if everyone around the world recognized the *Oneness* (at-one-ment) of their shared divinity with God. In his book and on the video of his PBS appearance that were offered as a premium to PBS subscribers, Dyer openly praised the teachings of *A Course in Miracles*. He and other New Age leaders were now clearly acknowledging that the New Age teachings of the Course are providing the spiritual undergirding for their *small groups* methodology for envisioning, affirming, and ultimately attaining their *dream* of world peace. In fact, Dyer told PBS viewers that the world would be a more peaceful place if everyone was living by the New Age principles of *A Course in Miracles*. He said:

> You know, I've been studying something for several years and the thing that I've been studying is called *A Course in Miracles*, and *A Course in Miracles* is a very interesting collection of brilliant writing that I think if the world were living by it perhaps we would have far, far, fewer of the conflicts and struggles and so on that we have amongst ourselves and amongst nations and in our families...[10]

After watching these Global Renaissance Alliance leaders stream across television with their similar sound bites, their advocacy of small groups, and their push for a world peace based on their New Age principles, I wrote in *Reinventing Jesus Christ*:

> For years now I have watched as "new age/new gospel" proponents like Marianne Williamson, Gary Zukav, Wayne Dyer, Barbara Marx Hubbard and others have introduced the "Christ" of the "new gospel" through their books and public appearances. But these [presentations] were usually theoretical and most of [these individuals] seemed only loosely identified with one another.
>
> Now, after September 11, everything is moving into a much clearer prophetic perspective. It is extremely sobering to watch as these same individuals emerge on prime-time television as part of a "global alliance" that is introducing their "new gospel" as a means of achieving world peace. Everything seems to be coming about as the "God" and "Christ" of the "new gospel" [are] starting to publicly introduce [their] "alternative to Armageddon" [PEACE Plan] as the only way to a true and lasting peace.[11]

Whose PEACE Plan?

The Bible warns its readers to beware of exchanging their souls for the purposes of the world (Mark 8:36-37) or for gaining a world peace that will be no real peace at all. But you never seem to hear any warnings about possible deception from Robert Schuller, Rick Warren or Bruce Wilkinson. They seem to focus only on what they consider to be "God's Dream" to "change the world." Somehow they seem to minimize the fact that Satan is described in the Bible as the extremely deceptive "god of this world" (2 Corinthians 4:4), and that he comes as an "angel of light" and his ministers as "ministers of righteousness" (2 Corinthians 11:14-15).

A young Rick Warren had read Robert Schuller's book *Your Church Has Real Possibilities*.[12] While still in seminary he and his wife drove all the way from Texas to California to attend Schuller's Institute for Successful Church Leadership. As a new pastor and a "graduate" of the Schuller Institute, he started his church within a half-hour of the Crystal Cathedral. Schuller's influence on the young pastor was pervasive and "profound." Schuller had recently boasted that Rick Warren had come to his Institute "time after time."[13]

Following Schuller's forty-year commitment to his church, Rick Warren made a forty-year commitment to the Saddleback community. He "grew" his mega-church by faithfully implementing all that he had learned from Schuller. His continued high esteem for Schuller is clearly evidenced by all of the non-referenced Schuller material that was surfacing in his book *The Purpose-Driven Life*. Now Schuller's concept of "God's Dream" was being used to inspire millions of Christians to get behind his 5-Step P.E.A.C.E. Plan to "change the world"—a 5-Step P.E.A.C.E. Plan that, on paper, bore an eerie resemblance to the 5-Step PEACE Plan proposed by Neale Donald Walsch and his New Age "God."

Chapter 13

Deceived about Deception

Concentrate on the positive.
If you accept Jesus Christ as your Savior
and take Him in your life,
you'll never have to worry about the devil.[1]

Robert Schuller
Discover Your Possibilities, 1978

It helps to know that Satan is entirely predictable.[2]

Rick Warren
The Purpose Driven Life, 2002

In Matthew 24:3, just prior to His crucifixion, the disciples asked Jesus what would be the sign of His coming and of the end of the world.

> And as he sat upon the mount of Olives, the disciples came unto him privately, saying, Tell us, when shall these things be? and what *shall be* the sign of thy coming, and of the end of the world?

His answer was direct and straightforward and provided tremendous prophetic detail. He began His lengthy and thorough discussion of prophetic signs by warning them first and foremost about the great deception that would be taking place on Earth prior to His return. He warned them: "Take heed that no man deceive you." Jesus then proceeded to give them over thirty verses describing the prophetic signs they could expect to see as the end draws near.

Among the many prophetic signs He described were:

the deceptive use of the name of Christ, false prophets, false signs and wonders, and the appearance of an ultimate false Christ—the Antichrist. Jesus warned that many people following Him, the true Christ, would be persecuted and killed.

Jesus also described the details of His own triumphant return. He assured His disciples that He would be coming in the heavens with power and great glory and that His justice would ultimately prevail. Yet, *throughout* His prophetic discourse, He warned of the *great deception* that would come at the time of the end. He told them that He warned them of these things ahead of time so they might take heed and not be deceived. Jesus told them to "watch" for these signs because no one except the Father knows the exact time of His return.

In *The Purpose-Driven Life*, Rick Warren asked the approximate question the disciples asked on the Mount of Olives. Except, instead of asking about the *signs* concerning Jesus' return and the end of the world as they did in Matthew 24, he limited his question solely to the *timing* of Jesus' return:

> Today there's a growing interest in the second coming of Christ and the end of the world. When will it happen? Just before Jesus ascended to heaven the disciples asked him this same question, and his response was quite revealing. He said, *"It is not for you to know the times or dates the Father has set by his own authority. But you will receive power when the Holy Spirit comes on you; and you will be my witnesses in Jerusalem, and in all Judea and Samaria, and to the ends of the earth."*[3] (Acts 1:7-8, NIV)

Focusing only on the single issue of timing in this one passage from the Book of Acts, Rick Warren has left the reader with the distinct impression that the prophetic details of Jesus' return are none of their business. He wrote:

> When the disciples wanted to talk about prophecy, Jesus
> quickly switched the conversation to evangelism. He
> wanted them to concentrate on their mission in the world.
> He said in essence, "The details of my return are none of
> your business. What *is* your business is the mission I've
> given you. Focus on that!"[4]

Having already given them tremendous amounts of prophetic detail on the Mount of Olives about the signs surrounding His return, Jesus would be contradicting himself if He were in any way implying that the details of His return were none of their business. On the Mount of Olives when the disciples wanted to talk about prophecy, did He quickly switch the conversation to evangelism? No. He gave them scripture after prophetic scripture detailing the signs that would precede His return and the end of the world. Jesus obviously believed prophecy *was* their business. The disciples wanted to know about signs, and they were given signs.

What is so ironic is that, in his effort to seemingly discourage his readers from studying and understanding prophecy, Rick Warren has to go back to the Mount of Olives and all of that explicit prophetic detail to try to make his point. The two scriptures he cites (Matthew 24:36; Matthew 24:14) are part of the over thirty verses of prophetic detail that Jesus was providing to His disciples so they would not be deceived in regards to His eventual return. Rick Warren wrote:

> Speculating on the exact timing of Christ's return is futile,
> because Jesus said, *"No one knows about that day or hour,
> not even the angels in heaven, nor the Son, but only the
> Father"* [Matthew 24:36, NIV]. Since Jesus said he didn't
> know the day or hour, why should you try to figure it out?
> What we *do* know for sure is this: Jesus will not return
> until everyone God wants to hear the Good News has
> heard it. Jesus said, *"The Good News about God's kingdom*

will be preached in all the world, to every nation. Then the
end will come" [Matthew 24:14, NCV]. If you want Jesus
to come back sooner, focus on fulfilling your mission, not
figuring out prophecy.[5]

The Matthew 24:36 verse that Rick Warren has cited in
regards to timing is actually part of all the prophetic detail
that Jesus freely and willingly gave to His disciples in
response to their question in Matthew 24:3: "Tell us, when
shall these things be? and what *shall be* the sign of thy
coming, and of the end of the world?" And the only reason
Rick Warren can cite Matthew 24:14 with prophetic authority when he says, "What we *do* know for sure," is because
the scripture he is quoting is one of the many prophetic
details Jesus provided on the Mount of Olives concerning
His return. And Rick Warren knows it "for sure" because it
was prophetic and *part of* all the other prophetic detail that
Jesus wanted His disciples to be aware of.

It is so clear from Jesus' whole discussion on the Mount
of Olives that He is telling His disciples, and all of us, that
an understanding of the details of His return is very important. He provides much needed prophetic information so
that His followers will not be deceived about the details of
His return at the end of time. He warns that there will be
false teachers and false teachings that will try to confuse the
details of His return. He provides the prophetic detail because He didn't want His disciples, or any of us, mistaking
Antichrist's arrival for His own return. He initiates His
lengthy prophetic discourse by saying, "Take heed that no
man deceive you." He ends His discussion by warning them
to "watch" and "be ready."

How could Rick Warren ever conclude, and tell his
millions of readers, that Jesus was informing His followers
that the details of His return were none of their business?

Details of Jesus' Return
Are Definitely Our Business

Coming out of New Age teachings, I had learned in a very personal way that the details of Jesus' return are definitely our business. Understanding the events surrounding His return was critical to understanding how badly I had been deceived by my New Age teachings. I had learned from reading the Bible that there is a false Christ on the horizon and that for a number of years I had unknowingly been one of his followers. Because the Bible's clear authoritative teachings about the real Jesus and His true return had been brought to my attention, I was able to see how deceived I was. By understanding that there is a false Christ trying to counterfeit the true Christ's return, I was able to renounce the false Christ I had been following and commit my life to the true Jesus Christ.

Jesus described the circumstances of His return in such prolific and exquisite detail because He knew that heavy spiritual deception would characterize the time of the end. I remember reading through Matthew 24 over and over again, along with all of the other scriptures that clearly described the great deception that would befall the world at the end of time. The passages in the Bible relating to spiritual deception and the detailing of Jesus' true return had helped save my life.

Somehow, Rick Warren and many of the men in Christian leadership just don't seem to get it. There is a false Christ who is very present on the world's scene, and he is coming right at the Church. This false Christ's top New Age leaders are unified, and they are in the process of trying to convert the world and the Church to the New Spirituality—a New Spirituality that is preparing the way for the arrival of their ultimate false "Christ."

Because Rick Warren and other church leaders don't

seem to discern the deception, they are unfortunately becoming a part of the deceptive process. Perhaps deceived into thinking that they can't be deceived, their inability to spiritually discern what is happening is placing the Church in grave danger. They don't seem to understand how our spiritual Adversary wants to use the Purpose-Driven Church for his own ulterior purposes.

Purpose as a Ploy

Even as I write, Neale Donald Walsch's New Age colleague Wayne Dyer is teaching the principles of the New Spirituality to an unsuspecting American public on a 3-hour PBS television special. His subject? The power of intention and purpose.[6] While Dyer was cleverly presenting the New Spirituality by talking about the power of "purpose," Rick Warren was judging a "Power of Purpose" essay contest for the New Age-based Templeton Foundation.[7] John Templeton—with his strong New Age and metaphysical leanings—believes in a "shared divinity between God and humanity."[8] Templeton has been featured on the cover of Robert Schuller's *Possibilities Magazine*,[9] and he was recently described as "my wonderful role model" by none other than Neale Donald Walsch.[10]

There is a false Christ on the world scene, and he is using "purpose" as a ploy to seduce the world into accepting the compromised principles of his New Spirituality. As Rick Warren and other Christian leaders remain in denial about all of this, only the prophetic detail of the Bible exposes this false Christ and his nefarious "purposes." Prophetic detail about end-time events is *definitely* our business.

Be Prepared for the Worst-Case Scenario

Years ago, when I was being interviewed on an Oregon radio station about my book *The Light that was Dark*, a caller asked my view concerning the timing of Christ's return. I told him that my view was simply this: that it is always best to be prepared for the worst-case scenario. I stated that there is no promise in Scripture that believers will escape the coming of Antichrist. I said that while there are widely varying views on the subject, it just seems to make a lot of sense to be prepared for the worst. An attitude of preparedness is totally consistent with the Bible's warnings to "put on the whole armour of God," and to "watch" and "be ready," and to not be "deceived" by *any* man.

But Rick Warren, and most Christian leaders today, are not talking about spiritual deception. They are not exposing the stepped-up New Age teachings that are now mainstream. They are not talking about the New Age PEACE Plan to merge biblical Christianity with the New Spirituality. They are not preparing believers for the worst-case scenario of the coming of Antichrist. Focusing instead on "God's Dream for the world," the Purpose-Driven Church is forgetting God's warning to the world. A mighty deceiver is coming with false prophets and false teachings and "all power and signs and lying wonders" to convince the world that he is the Christ (2 Thessalonians 2:3-9). In fact, it is not impossible that this ultimate deceiver is already in the world today. Take Maitreya, for example.

Chapter 14

False Christ with a Purpose

I am your Purpose.[1]

I am your Hope.[2]

I am your Heart.[3]

God is within you and all around you.[4]

My name is Oneness.[5]

I shall place before you all the purpose of God.[6]

My Plan is God's Plan.[7]

Nothing will happen by chance.[8]

Take part in a Great Plan which is changing
the world...[9]

My Coming brings peace.[10]

Maitreya the "Christ"
Messages from Maitreya the Christ, 1992

There is a false Christ claiming that he is already in the world today and that he is simply waiting for humanity to call him forth. He, too, has "a purpose" and is "purpose driven." He has a peace plan and says that his coming will bring peace. He puts a premium on service to mankind, and he has a plan to help the lost and the sick and the poor. He is a prototype for Antichrist and still remains a viable candidate for being *the* Antichrist. His teachings are consistent with the New Age teachings of the New Spirituality. The Bible has warned us that someday he, or someone like him, will be everyone's "worst-case scenario" come true. He, or someone like him, will turn everyone's grandest dreams into a total nightmare. Thus, it behooves all of us to at least be minimally alert to someone who so nearly fits the Bible's warnings—especially when his teachings so closely parallel the teachings of the New Spirituality.

This particular false Christ figure is Maitreya "the Christ." He describes himself not as the world "savior" but, rather, as the "World Teacher." He has maintained contact with the world through his longtime chief spokesperson, English artist and "esotericist" Benjamin Creme. Maitreya's future role as the returning "Christ" is described by Creme in his 1980 book, *The Reappearance of the Christ and the Masters of Wisdom.* Another spokesperson, Wayne Peterson, has written a more recent book entitled *Extraordinary Times, Extraordinary Beings: Experiences of an American Diplomat with Maitreya and the Masters of Wisdom.* In his 2001 book, Wayne Peterson wrote about Maitreya's role with the world's major religions:

> He is the one awaited by all the major religions albeit unknown to them. The Christians wait for the return of the Christ, Buddhists for the next Buddha, Muslims for the Imam Mahdi, Hindus for a reincarnation of Krishna, and the Jews for the Messiah. These are all different names for one individual, Maitreya, who is here not as a religious leader but as a teacher for *all* humanity.[11]

Wayne Peterson described what he learned from Benjamin Creme about Maitreya's purpose:

> Maitreya's purpose, Creme indicated, was to help us realize our innate divinity through learning to live in right relationship as brothers and sisters of one great family. The first step was to establish sharing as the way to eliminate the poverty and starvation that caused millions around the

world to die daily in the midst of plenty. Maitreya was emerging in time to help us save ourselves and the planet, and would make himself known to all in a televised 'Day of Declaration' soon to come.[12]

Maitreya has reportedly been living anonymously in the Western world since 1977. His "return" and presence here on earth was announced in full page newspaper ads in major cities around the world in 1982. He has an unofficial world organization entitled "Share International," and his followers have been reported by Creme and Peterson to include many prominent world figures, including Mikhail Gorbachev[13] and Nelson Mandela.[14]

Maitreya has made it known that when he returns twelve "Masters of Wisdom" will accompany him to help "teach" humanity the "New Truth"[15] and the "new way."[16] In what would prove to be a most clever device, he has stated that one of these "Masters" will be "Jesus,"—a "Master Jesus"—who is not Jesus Christ but a "disciple" of "the Christ." Maitreya has made it clear that he, Maitreya, is the only person occupying the "office" of "Christ," that he has occupied that "office" for over 2600 years, and that it was he as the "Christ" who "overshadowed" and worked through Jesus, the man, in Palestine back in the first century. Benjamin Creme explained:

> In the esoteric tradition, the Christ is not the name of an individual but of an Office in the Hierarchy. The present holder of that Office, the Lord Maitreya, has held it for 2,600 years, and manifested in Palestine through His Disciple, Jesus, by the occult method of overshadowing, the most frequent form used for the manifestation of Avatars. He has never left the world, but for 2,000 years has waited and planned for this immediate future time, training His Disciples, and preparing Himself for the awesome task which awaits Him. He has made it known that this time, He Himself will come.[17]

Overlapping "Purposes"

*I*t is worth noting that Maitreya's most significant New Age teachings about hope, purpose, dreams, destiny, service, peace and the idea that God is "in" everything overlap in significant ways with many of the words and teachings of Robert Schuller and Rick Warren. These areas of overlap are starting to blur some of the crucial differences between biblical Christianity and the New Spirituality. The reason the blurring is starting to occur is because Robert Schuller, Rick Warren, and most Christian leaders make no effort to distinguish the difference between what they are saying and what false Christs, like Maitreya, and the New Spirituality are saying. For example, Maitreya, like Rick Warren, is very fond of the word "purpose"—he uses it all the time. Maitreya has proclaimed to all humanity:

> We are together, you and I, for the same purpose.[18]

> Take My hand, My friends, and let us together walk that Path and know the meaning of Life, know the blessing of Love, know the purpose of God.[19]

> I need all those who long to serve, who wish to fulfil their purpose in life...[20]

> I shall place before you all the purpose of God.[21]

> Hold fast to My Purpose, which is to take man to God.[22]

> My Purpose unfolds.[23]

> My Purposes are being fulfilled.[24]

> I am your Purpose.[25]

Occupying the whole back cover of the book *Messages*

from Maitreya is "The Great Invocation." According to Benjamin Creme, this invocation was introduced into the world by Maitreya and is now commonly recited in New Age-oriented churches around the world. "The Great Invocation" invokes the return of "the Christ" and calls for a restoration of "The Plan." The middle lines of the Invocation specifically invoke God's "purpose."

> From the centre where the Will of God is known
> Let purpose guide the little wills of men—
> The purpose which the Masters know and serve.

Creme explained why Maitreya released "The Great Invocation" to humanity:

> to enable man himself to invoke the energies which would change our world, and make possible the return of the Christ and Hierarchy.[26]

Maitreya's deceptive "purpose" as the "World Teacher" is to convince everyone they are divine. His plan is to teach humanity to believe in the "immanent" nature of God; that is, that God is "in" everyone, so everyone is divine.

Immanence: the "God" Within

Familiar with much of the material on Maitreya, I suddenly found myself looking at him in a whole new way after reading Rick Warren and Robert Schuller. There was something very disturbing about the similarity of their teachings, especially in regards to "purpose" and the idea that God is "in" everyone and everything.

On page 88 of *The Purpose-Driven Life*, Rick Warren wrote:

Because God is with you all the time, no place is any closer to God than the place where you are right now. The Bible says, *"He rules everything and is everywhere and is in everything."*

On page 88 in *Messages from Maitreya the Christ*, Maitreya is quoted as saying:

My friends, God is nearer to you than you can imagine.
God is yourself.
God is within you and all around you.

On page 88 of his book *The Reappearance of the Christ and the Masters of Wisdom*, Benjamin Creme explained Maitreya's "new world religion." He described the same "immanent" aspect of God that Rick Warren was conveying with his *New Century Version* of Ephesians 4:6:

But eventually a new world religion will be inaugurated which will be a fusion and synthesis of the approach of the East and the approach of the West. The Christ will bring together, not simply Christianity and Buddhism, but the concept of God transcendent—outside of His creation— and also the concept of God immanent in all creation—in man and all creation.

Renowned occult teacher and New Age Theosophist Alice A. Bailey also described how a new world religion will be based on this "immanent" aspect of God. Emphasizing the word *"fresh,"* she states that the "Path to God" will be based on:

...a **fresh orientation** to divinity and to the acceptance of the fact of God Transcendent and of God Immanent within every form of life.

These are the foundational truths upon which the world religion of the future will rest.[27] (Emphasis added)

This same "immanent" aspect of God so important to Maitreya, Alice A. Bailey, the New Spirituality and the New World Religion is also very important to Rick Warren. This idea of "immanence" is taught as part of the *Foundations* course at Rick Warren's Saddleback Church. Echoing Bailey's use of the word "**fresh**," the *Foundations Participant's Guide* under the section heading "**A Fresh Word**" reiterates Rick Warren's teaching that God is "in" everything. It states:

> The fact that God stands above and beyond his creation does not mean he stands outside his creation. He is both transcendent (above and beyond his creation) and immanent (within and throughout his creation).[28] (Parentheses in original)

Robert Schuller has also stressed this aspect of immanence. In a November 9, 2003 sermon at the Crystal Cathedral, Robert Schuller stated that God was not only transcendent but also immanent. He said that as a result of his becoming more aware of the immanence of God, his faith was now "deeper, broader, and richer more than ever." As previously cited, he summarized what he meant by the immanence of God by telling his worldwide television audience:

> **Yes, God is alive and He is in every single human being!**[29]

Also, as previously mentioned in Chapter Three of this book, this "immanent" aspect of God is also evident in Rick Warren's favored paraphrase, Eugene Peterson's *The Message*. The notion that God is "in" everything and is "One" with creation is contained in the magical saying "as above, so below." This is the mystical New Age phrase that Eugene Peterson injected in its entirety into the Lord's Prayer and in its derivative form into Colossians 1:16—the verse that

Rick Warren used to introduce his readers to *The Purpose-Driven Life.* As previously cited, the editors of the *New Age Journal* described this immanent aspect of God and its New Age significance in their book *As Above, So Below*:

> "As above, so below; as below, so above." This maxim implies that the transcendent God beyond the physical universe and the immanent God within ourselves are one.[30]

The spiritual implications of all of these overlapping statements are enormous. Rick Warren, Robert Schuller, and Eugene Peterson are all now teaching this immanent aspect of God—that God is "in" everyone. On this critical theological point, these particular Christian leaders are not only *not exposing* one of the central concepts of the "New Spirituality" and probable New World Religion—they seem to be *agreeing with it!*

A friend of mine who used to go to Saddleback Church came over to the house one night to try to demonstrate that Rick Warren wasn't deceived about the New Age or about spiritual deception. I knew his argument would be based on the fact that Rick Warren had made a statement in *The Purpose-Driven Life* that said we will never become God and that we are not divine. He had even used the term "New Age philosophies."[31] Before my friend could even begin to make his point, I had him turn to page 88 in *The Purpose-Driven Life.* I read the passage out loud:

> Because God is with you all the time, no place is any closer to God than the place where you are right now. The Bible says, *"He rules everything and is everywhere and is in everything."*

My friend hung his head in disbelief and then exclaimed, "That's pantheism!" He had immediately grasped the dangerous New Age implications of what Rick Warren was saying. He understood that whatever New Age disclaimers Rick Warren seemed to be making, he had just overridden them by what he was actually teaching. On the one hand, Rick Warren has proclaimed that humans are not divine, yet he opens the door to this New Spirituality belief by proclaiming that God is "in" everything. This same friend told me on another occasion that he had never been taught anything meaningful about spiritual deception while attending Saddleback Church.

"Master Jesus" and the New Reformation

Unless Rick Warren and other church leaders start to really expose the New Age, by delineating the differences between biblical Christianity and the New Spirituality, there will be real confusion down the line. Successful coaches have their teams as fully prepared as possible for whatever the opposition may have up their sleeve—including last minute trick plays at the end of the game. Christian leaders must do the same.

It is imperative that the Church be prepared for a false Christ figure like Maitreya suddenly appearing and presenting himself as "the Christ" and proclaiming the *immanence* of God "in" everyone and everything. It could happen. We cannot afford to be complacent. We must not be ignorant of our Adversary's schemes and devices (2 Corinthians 2:11).

For example, Benjamin Creme, as previously mentioned, has tried to convince us that Jesus is *not* the Christ but rather a disciple of Maitreya "the Christ." He explained that in the first century Jesus allowed Maitreya to "overshadow" and work through him after he was baptized.

> He was, and still is, a Disciple of the Christ and made the great sacrifice of giving up His body for the use of the Christ. By the occult process of overshadowing, the Christ,

Wrong   Wrong

Maitreya, took over and worked through the body of Jesus
from the Baptism onwards.[32]

and Wrong again

Creme explained that when Maitreya reveals himself as
"Christ," he will be joined by "twelve Masters of Wisdom"
who help him do his work in the world. Creme has stated
that "Jesus" will be one of these "Masters" returning with
Maitreya. But according to Creme, this "Jesus" is *not* the
Lord and he is *not* the Christ—he is a "Master" and a
"Master" only. Creme claims that Maitreya is the Lord and
Christ. Creme has explained that the "Master Jesus" will be
serving the "Lord Maitreya" by assuming the throne of St.
Peter in Rome and heading up "the Christian Church." This
"Master Jesus"—obviously a false Jesus—will be in charge
of a new reformation. It will be his job to "reform the
Christian churches."

> The Master Jesus is going to reform the Christian
> churches.[33]

> He will seek to transform the Christian Churches, in so far
> as they are flexible enough to respond correctly to the new
> reality which the return of the Christ and the Masters will
> create.[34]

Sadly, many of the newer Bible translations and
paraphrases used by Rick Warren have often dropped the
words "Lord" and "Christ" from Jesus' title and have
substituted the word "Master." This obviously plays directly
into the hands of a false Christ, like Maitreya, who will be
trying to convince the world—and particularly Christians—that Jesus is *not* the Lord Jesus Christ but simply the
"Master Jesus."

Also favorable to Maitreya are the new versions'
frequent use of the word "Teacher" in conjunction with the
term "Christ." Maitreya presents himself not as the world

"savior" but as the "World Teacher." The frequent associa-
tion of the word "Teacher" with Christ, in new versions like
The Message, seems to underscore and give validity to
Maitreya's role as "Christ" and "World Teacher." Interest-
ingly, the word "Teacher" is directly associated with Jesus
Christ only one time in the *King James* translation of the
Gospels. It appears at least twenty-five times in *The Message*
paraphrase of the Gospels.

And while the disciples and followers of the real Jesus
called Him "Master," it was always with the understanding
that He was also their "Lord" and "Christ." But in the *King
James Bible*, when they addressed Him as "Master" they
never—not even once—directly addressed Him as "Master
Jesus." Yet, the term "Master Jesus" appears repeatedly in
Eugene Peterson's *The Message*. Peterson continually drops
the word "Lord" from Jesus' title, choosing instead to refer
to Him as "Master Jesus."

For example, the *King James* translation of Revelation
22:20-21 at the very end of the Bible is:

> Even so, come, Lord Jesus.
> The grace of our Lord Jesus Christ *be* with you all. Amen.

The Message paraphrase is:

> Yes! Come, Master Jesus!
> The grace of the Master Jesus be with all of you. Oh, Yes![35]

Maitreya's hope is that most people calling themselves
Christians will be content to follow the lead of his false
"Master Jesus" who will be in charge of "reforming" the
"Christian" Church—a "Christian" Church that regards
Maitreya, not Jesus, as their Lord and Christ. As a proto-
type, Maitreya is a perfect example of how the eventual
Antichrist might attempt to deceive the world. Exposing

Maitreya's "Master Jesus" scheme and his "new reformation" scheme—as the Bible admonishes us to do (Ephesians 5:11-13)—would be a good way for Rick Warren and other Christian leaders to prepare believers for a possible "worst-case scenario" of having someone like Maitreya suddenly appearing and claiming to be Christ.

Robert Schuller, Rick Warren and other Christian leaders need to make a clear distinction between their call for a "new reformation" and the one called for by Neale Donald Walsch and the false Christ, Maitreya. Sadly, Rick Warren seems to be completely unaware of the overlapping implications of his 5-Step P.E.A.C.E. Plan and the 5-Step PEACE Plan proposed by Neale Donald Walsch and his New Age "God." Both of their PEACE Plans use the word PEACE as an acronym. Both of the PEACE Plans proclaim they will "change the world" and "change history." Both of the PEACE Plans describe themselves as "God's Plan" and emphatically declare that God is in the process of bringing "peace" to the world. And both of these 5-Step PEACE Plans call for a "new reformation." A "new reformation" that, with a few deceptive twists and turns, could be overseen by a "Master Jesus" who is not the real Jesus Christ. A "Master Jesus" who teaches that we are all divine because God is "in" everything.

Persecution Through the "Selection Process"

But while Maitreya talks of "love" and "peace" and the *one family* of mankind, he has issued a very strict warning to those people who persist in remaining "separate" by refusing to see themselves and everyone else as "divine." He has warned that those who refuse to accept the doctrine of immanence and *Oneness*—humanity's shared divinity with God—will be selectively expelled from the human race. Specifically using the terms "purpose" and "driven," this

Purpose Driven false Christ has declared that it is his "purpose" to make sure that anyone who remains "separate," by denying the divinity of man, be "driven" from this planet.

> All that hinders the manifestation of man's divinity must be driven from our planet.[36]

> The crime of separation must be driven from this world. I affirm that as My Purpose.[37]

New Age leader Barbara Marx Hubbard, who is on the board of Directors of The Global Renaissance Alliance and is a speaker for Walsch's Humanity's Team, wrote that she was told the same thing. Hubbard stated that her "Christ" specifically described this purposeful elimination process as "the selection process." Like Maitreya, she stated that the selection process will be the penalty for anyone who persists in the "self-centered" belief that humanity is not divine and is "separate" from God. By this definition, Bible-believing Christians—the ones who *really are* Bible believing—would be defined as among those who are "self-centered" and "separate." In what would be a fulfillment of the prophecy that the Antichrist will "make war with the saints" (Revelation 13:7), Hubbard's "Christ"—sounding much like Maitreya—states that he will "make war" on those who are "fearful" and "self-centered."

> [T]he fundamental regression is self-centeredness, or the illusion that you are separate from God. I "make war" on self-centeredness. It shall surely be overcome. The child must become the adult. Human must become Divine. That is the law.[38]

> At the co-creative stage of evolution, one self-centered soul is like a lethal cancer cell in a body: deadly to itself and to the whole.[39]

The surgeon dare leave no cancer in the body when he closes up the wound after a delicate operation. We dare leave no self-centeredness on Earth after the selection process.[40]

The future implications of all this are obviously very ominous for the so-called "fearful" Christians who refuse to believe in the false doctrine of immanence and *Oneness*— humanity's shared divinity with God—and who continue to profess that Jesus Christ is their Lord and Savior. In *Reinventing Jesus Christ: The New Gospel,* I warned:

In the [New Age] "new gospel" [New Spirituality] scheme of things, "fear" means seeing yourself and your fellow man as "separate" and not as a part of God. "Fear" and "separation" are equated with all of those who refuse to see themselves as being a part of God…."Fear" and "separation" prevent the attainment of peace, produce illness in the body of mankind, and prevent spiritual growth. They are the ticket to the "selection process" because they prevent the "one body" of humanity from advancing to the next spiritual level. "Fear" and "separation" people are those who oppose "new gospel" teachings and the "new gospel" God and Christ….

How do "God" and "Christ" suggest that Christians, and others under "the illusion of separation," rid themselves of the "fear" that is causing them to feel separate from God? By "atoning" through the "at-one-ment" process. That is, by affirming that "all is love" and "all is God" and never forgetting that they are a part of God. By "new gospel" definition, the only way you can be "loving" and "at-one" with your fellow man is by ultimately pledging allegiance to the doctrine of "oneness."….In the "new gospel" future you will live or die based on whether or not you see yourself as a part of God. It is the doctrine of "oneness" versus the doctrine of "separation." It is as simple and straightforward and brutal as that….

The upshot of this clever conditioning process is to

impress people everywhere with the seemingly indisput-
able contention that if you are against "oneness" you are
also against God, Christ, and your fellow man.

Only an ingenious and creatively deceptive spirit world
could have thought up such a diabolical way of separating
and disparaging Christian believers and others who do not
believe they are a part of God. Who could possibly be
against "oneness"? And the answer is, of course, only
those who have been "deceived" into believing in the
"crime of separation."[41]

In a possible worst-case scenario with someone like
Maitreya declaring himself to be "the Christ," faithful
Christians would know that Maitreya is *not* the Christ and
that his "Master Jesus" is *not* the real Jesus. Denying them
both and refusing to accept the false doctrine of Oneness,
Christians would immediately be branded as "fearful,"
"separate," "self-centered," and "exclusivistic" for insisting
that Jesus is the Christ and their one and only Savior.
Believers would literally be "hated" for holding fast to the
name of the Lord Jesus Christ. And, in Maitreya's world, by
holding fast to the true Jesus Christ believers would face
certain death from the "selection process." Horrific as all of
this may be, it is consistent with Jesus' prophetic warnings
about Antichrist and the time of the end foretold in Scripture:

Then shall they deliver you up to be afflicted, and shall kill
you: and ye shall be hated of all nations for my name's
sake. (Matthew 24:9)

And it was given unto him to make war with the saints,
and to overcome them: and power was given him over all
kindreds, and tongues, and nations. (Revelation 13:7)

A true Bible-believer in Maitreya's world could, in
reality, be a loving, giving, peaceful person. But, by Maitre-

ya's definition and the definition of the New Spirituality, this believer would automatically be labeled as "self-centered" and subject to death by the "selection process." Again, this is precisely the kind of scenario that Jesus warned would happen at the time of the end.

A *choice* looms ahead for mankind. According to the New Spirituality, those who are not "separate" and "self-centered" are those who believe that "we are all One" because God is "in" everything. They will evolve and live on in the New Age. Those who refuse to accept the "imma-nent" view that God is "in" everything and that we are all "One" will be handed over to the "selection process." If Rick Warren and those in Christian leadership don't start spelling out the differences between biblical Christianity and the New Spirituality, the Purpose-Driven Church could end up getting very deceived. The Bible is very clear that in the future many people describing themselves as Christians will be deceived into abandoning Jesus as their Lord and Christ and will end up following someone like Maitreya as their "Lord" and "Christ." In my book *Reinventing Jesus Christ: The New Gospel*, I warned:

> Somehow, Christians don't seem to grasp Jesus' warnings about the tremendous deception that characterizes the time of the end. Perhaps deceived into thinking that we can't be deceived, we don't take seriously enough His warnings that a Hitler-like antichrist figure will one day rise to rule the world—and that many people calling them-selves "Christians" will support this spiritual counterfeit who will actually come in the name of Christ. Our adver-sary wants us to believe that these warnings are for another people at another time. Yet through Scripture, and in our heart of hearts, the Spirit of God tells us that they are not. As we study the Bible, and as we watch and pray and observe the events all around us, we come to under-stand that these future times described by Jesus are now suddenly and undeniably upon us.[42]

Chapter 15

Contend for the Faith

Beloved, when I gave all diligence to write unto you of the common salvation, it was needful for me to write unto you, and exhort you that ye should earnestly contend for the faith which was once delivered unto the saints.

Jude 3

All I can say, after reading *The Purpose-Driven Life*, is that Rick Warren does not speak for me. He may be sincere. He may be well-intentioned. But I believe, with every fiber of my being, that he is in the process of leading the Church into the New Age plan for the New Spirituality. I recognize the spirit that seems to be influencing him because I once was influenced by it myself. It is a spirit that convinces us that we are doing God's will when we follow its leading. It is a spirit that convinces us that God is "in" everything and that world peace is just around the corner. It is a spirit that hides behind the banner of *God's purposes* while it tries to deceive us into accomplishing *its purposes*. It is a spirit that manipulates us into thinking we're one thing, while it makes us into something else. It is the spirit that leads Neale Donald Walsch and his Global Renaissance Alliance of New Age leaders. It is a spirit that comes in the name of Christ but actually opposes Jesus Christ.

The Bible warned us about all of this. The Apostle Paul was amazed that the Church in Galatia was starting to accept a new gospel that wasn't the true Gospel.

> I marvel that ye are so soon removed from him that called
> you into the grace of Christ unto another gospel: Which is
> not another; but there be some that trouble you, and
> would pervert the gospel of Christ. (Galatians 1:6-7)

Paul warned that if *anyone*—whether an angel from heaven or even a trusted leader like himself—introduced the false teachings of "another gospel," this person should be completely disregarded.

> But though we, or an angel from heaven, preach any other
> gospel unto you than that which we have preached unto
> you, let him be accursed. As we said before, so say I now
> again, If any *man* preach any other gospel unto you than
> that ye have received, let him be accursed.
> (Galatians 1:8-9)

He told them that if he was only trying to please men, he wouldn't be the servant of Christ.

> For do I now persuade men, or God? or do I seek to please
> men? for if I yet pleased men, I should not be the servant
> of Christ. (Galatians 1:10)

Paul warned the wayward Corinthian Church that "another spirit" *not from God* could work through men claiming to follow Jesus. He warned them that they were spiritually vulnerable, and just gullible enough, to be led by that spirit to follow "another Jesus" and "another gospel."

> For if he that cometh preacheth another Jesus, whom we
> have not preached, or *if* ye receive another spirit, which ye
> have not received, or another gospel, which ye have not
> accepted, ye might well bear with *him*.
> (2 Corinthians 11:4)

Paul was warning of deceptive false Christs, like

Maitreya, who would present "another Jesus"—like the "Master Jesus"—who would not be the real Jesus Christ. The true Jesus Christ warned His disciples that there would be many—like those in the New Age and the New Spirituality—who would also claim to be Christ.

> And Jesus answered and said unto them, Take heed that no man deceive you. For many shall come in my name, saying, I am Christ; and shall deceive many. (Matthew 24: 4-5)

The true Jesus Christ also warned that on Judgment Day many people calling themselves Christians, and claiming to have done "wonderful works" in Jesus' name, will be utterly shocked to find out that they had been following "another spirit," "another Jesus," and "another gospel."

> Not every one that saith unto me, Lord, Lord, shall enter into the kingdom of heaven; but he that doeth the will of my Father which is in heaven. Many will say to me in that day, Lord, Lord, have we not prophesied in thy name? and in thy name have cast out devils? and in thy name done many wonderful works? And then will I profess unto them, I never knew you: depart from me, ye that work iniquity. (Matthew 7:21-23)

The Bible elaborates on Jesus' already extensive warnings about spiritual deception. The Apostle Paul explicitly stated that he had been impressed by the Holy Spirit to warn the Church that in the last days people would depart from the true Christian faith because they would be led by "seducing spirits" and false doctrines—not by the Holy Spirit of the one true God.

> Now the Spirit speaketh expressly, that in the latter times some shall depart from the faith, giving heed to seducing spirits, and doctrines of devils. (1 Timothy 4:1)

He said that people would accept teachings and doctrines that were not from God because they would find teachers who would tell them what they wanted to hear. He warned that these false teachers would turn people away from the truth.

> For the time will come when they will not endure sound doctrine; but after their own lusts shall they heap to themselves teachers, having itching ears; And they shall turn away *their* ears from the truth, and shall be turned unto fables. (2 Timothy 4:3-4)

Paul warned that in the last days false teachers and false teachings would have the appearance of godliness but would lack the authentic power that comes from the Holy Spirit of the one true God. He warned believers to turn away from these false teachers and false teachings.

> Having a form of godliness, but denying the power thereof: from such turn away. (2 Timothy 3:5)

John specifically warned that people who abandon the truth of sound doctrine abandon Christ and God.

> Whosoever transgresseth, and abideth not in the doctrine of Christ, hath not God. He that abideth in the doctrine of Christ, he hath both the Father and the Son. If there come any unto you, and bring not this doctrine, receive him not into *your* house, neither bid him God speed: For he that biddeth him God speed is partaker of his evil deeds. (2 John 9-11)

Scripture is very clear how all this deception begins. It can begin with an erroneous false teaching like God is "in" everything. This false teaching can then open the door to other false teachings and even deeper deception. This is how people calling themselves Christians may one day be deceived into believing that we are all divine and "we are all One." Open that door a little wider and people may believe that we are all God—which is precisely what the serpent was tempting Eve to believe in the Garden of Eden when he claimed, "Ye shall be as gods." Paul warned us that it only takes a *little* leaven to completely change and distort the true Gospel of Jesus Christ.

> Ye did run well; who did hinder you that ye should not obey the truth? This persuasion cometh not of him that calleth you. A little leaven leaveneth the whole lump. (Galatians 5:7-9)

More than a Little Leaven 5

Make no mistake about it. The Purpose-Driven Church campaign to enlist every man, woman and child into its ranks to "do" the P.E.A.C.E. Plan and to "do" God's Dream did not have its origins at Saddleback Church or in the singly inspired mind of Rick Warren. What I had discovered in my reading was that the spiritual foundation of this whole Purpose-Driven movement could be found in the writings and teachings of Robert Schuller's 50-year ministry. While Rick Warren, Bruce Wilkinson and other Christian leaders and organizations forge new Purpose-Driven alliances around the world, the real architect of this seemingly unsinkable Purpose-Driven ship sits quietly in his office at the Crystal Cathedral—the same office where *A Course in Miracles* had once been shelved, and where Ernest Holmes' New Age text *Science of Mind* had been discreetly tucked away in a bottom desk drawer.

An acquaintance wondered if I was treating Rick Warren unfairly by linking him so closely with Robert Schuller. "After all," he argued, "Rick Warren is bringing a lot of people into the church. There is a real excitement about the Gospel and huge numbers of people are 'coming to the Lord.' Even if he has accepted some of Schuller's questionable teachings, look at all the good he is doing."

What immediately came to mind when he made that statement was the illustrative example I had heard so often when I first came into the faith: a glass of water that is 99% water and 1% arsenic will still kill you 100%. And trying to be "positive" by seeing the half-full, rather than half-empty glass, doesn't work with arsenic-tinged water. You will still die if there is even a little arsenic in what you are drinking. The Bible holds to the same principle in regards to doctrine. Doctrine that has been tinged with even the slightest bit of untruth can ultimately result in great deception. That is why the Bible severely warns that even "a little leaven leaveneth the whole lump." And that is why Jesus specifically warned us to beware of the "leaven" of *false doctrine* that can be taught by one's religious leaders (Matthew 16:11-12).

I told my acquaintance, who was trying to be "positive," that the Bible is clear that truth cannot be mixed with untruth or half-truth in bringing people to the Lord. That's how people end up spiritually deceived. It's how I ended up with the "God" and "Jesus" and "Holy Spirit" of the New Age. And that is how the Church is starting to involve itself with the New Age teachings of the New Spirituality without even knowing it. That is why it is so important that we test the truth of any teaching that presents itself in the name of God. The Bible tells us to refuse anything that is not in accord with Scripture because "a little leaven" can change everything. I had learned from my own deceptive experience that once the door to false teachings is opened ever so slightly, it just keeps opening wider and wider.

When it comes to teaching about the things of God, nobody gets a free pass—not even Rick Warren. We are all accountable to truth. We must preach the whole truth and nothing but the truth. We cannot overlook *any* false teach-

ing or dismiss godly criticism by pointing out all the perceived good that seems to be coming from our "good works"
or whatever else we are doing. Jesus never operated this
way, and He doesn't want us to either. If we look at the
example of the arsenic tinged glass of water and believe the
Bible's warning that "a little leaven leaveneth the whole
lump," then we must also look at The Purpose-Driven Life and
any other book or teaching in this same way. A "little"
arsenic can kill any of the possible good that might come
from drinking that water. And a "little" leaven can kill any
of the possible good that can come from The Purpose-Driven
Life. And what I discovered is that there is more than a little
leaven in what Rick Warren is teaching.

In fact, his teaching that God is "in" everything is
leaven enough to "drive" his whole Purpose-Driven Church
into the New Spirituality. It is the kind of leaven that wins
the praise of the world and makes a false Christ like Maitreya smile. It is the kind of leaven that will open the door to
the very kind of interfaith "dialogue" that Neale Donald
Walsch and his New Age "God" so desperately desire. It is
the kind of leaven that is already in the process of leading
the Church into great delusion.

Certainly "guilt by association" is not a fair way to deal
with anyone. Jesus was falsely accused simply because He
associated with a wide variety of people. But His association
with these people didn't change who He was. It was He who
changed them. Can we say the same thing about the relationship between Rick Warren and Robert Schuller? From all
of my extensive reading it had become very clear to me that
it was Rick Warren who had the "itching ears." He was the
one who had been profoundly changed by his association
with Robert Schuller—not the other way around. The
Purpose-Driven Life had demonstrated to me that Rick
Warren wasn't so much presenting the teachings of Rick
Warren as he was the writings and teachings of Robert

Schuller. His association with Schuller was unmistakable and real.

In 1982, Robert Schuller called for a "new reformation" of the Church.[1] Today, Rick Warren is calling for a "new reformation" of the Church.[2] In 1982, Robert Schuller described God's plan to change and redeem the world as "God's Dream."[3] Today, Rick Warren presents a P.E.A.C.E. Plan that he describes as "God's Dream" to change the world.[4] In 1969, Robert Schuller wrote that "God lives in people."[5] Today, Rick Warren is teaching that God is "in" everything.[6] Rick Warren's use of Schuller's thoughts, ideas, teachings, words, and phrases—many of which I have already discussed—go on and on.

Rick Warren is not the "victim" of any "guilt by association." His relationship with Schuller has been an association by choice. Rick Warren went to Schuller. He made the choice to associate with Schuller and to adopt his teachings. It is in the adoption of those Schuller teachings that Rick Warren proves himself.

Bible commentator Matthew Henry rightly insists that the "fruits" of anyone's ministry include the "fruits of their doctrine."[7] And, in that regard, the "fruits" of Rick Warren's teachings and doctrine were proving themselves to be remarkably similar to the teachings and doctrine of Robert Schuller. Jesus said, "By their fruits ye shall know them" (Matthew 7:20). What I had learned in reading *The Purpose-Driven Life* was that, in regard to "fruits" and in regard to Rick Warren's relationship with Robert Schuller, the Rick Warren apple had not fallen all that far from the Robert Schuller tree.

Not Going Back to the New Age

I came out of the New Age. I am not about to go back into those New Age/new gospel teachings. I am not about to *me Too!*

become a part of the New Spirituality or whatever else they may call it tomorrow, I see the spiritual trap that has been laid out for the world—particularly for those of us who call ourselves believers. Jesus warned us that these days would come and it looks like these days are here. It is a very challenging time to be a believer. It is so important that we hold fast to the truth of the Bible lest we get talked out of that truth and let it "slip" away (Hebrews 2:1). If there was ever a time to stand fast in the truth, that time is now.

God is not in the process of doing something "new." He is not in the process of changing what we believe by suddenly "enlarging" our faith to make it compatible with the principles of a New Spirituality. No, that is what our spiritual adversaries would have us believe. That is what Neale Donald Walsch, his Global Renaissance Alliance of New Age leaders, and his Humanity's Team is all about. Yet, as the popularity of their New Age/new gospel teachings continues to exponentially increase, the Church has become strangely silent about what is going on. In *Reinventing Jesus Christ: The New Gospel*, I observed:

> Traditional Christian believers frequently mention the analogy of the frog that is so slowly and gradually boiled in a kettle of water that it dies before ever realizing what is going on. Yet many believers fail to realize that the very same thing is happening to them as they tell that story. How else do you explain the rapid rise of the [New Age] "new gospel" [New Spirituality] movement with hardly a word of concern within the Church about what's been happening? As [New Age] "new gospel" advocates continue to publish bestselling books and flock to the airwaves in ever-increasing numbers to advance their cause, there is a strange silence in Christendom. Does the Church have any idea what is going on?[8]

I have watched for over twenty years as deceived

Christian leaders have only given "lip service" to the dangers of New Age teachings, while they are out pursuing some "new" thing they perceive God is doing to "bless" the Church. Invariably, this "new" thing distracts everyone's attention from the spiritual deception that is in the world and in the Church. Somehow, today's Purpose-Driven Church has forgotten that Jesus' main "purpose" for coming into the world was to confront and defeat evil.

> For this purpose the Son of God was manifested, that he might destroy the works of the devil. (I John 3:8)

I was eventually saved when someone cared enough to explain how the true Jesus Christ had defeated the Devil and his works on the cross of Calvary. I was saved because someone cared enough to share important passages from the Bible that warned about spiritual deception and the evil that was in my midst. I was saved because I was told how to call upon the victory that Jesus had already won over sin and evil and death. I was made to understand that I was living in a world that was "hell-bent" on establishing its own "God" and "Christ" and eliminating all those who refused to play by its rules. But that isn't a very popular message in today's "post-modern" 21st century church that seems to be more intent on compromising the faith than on contending for it.

What goes through the minds of our Christian leaders when they hear that the "God" of the New Age and the New Spirituality is publicly proclaiming that "the era of the Single Savior is over?" What are they thinking when New Age leaders and false Christs, like Maitreya, nonchalantly describe a "selection process" that will kill those who persist in calling Jesus Christ their Lord and Savior? What kind of "leadership" is it that stays in denial and refuses to expose these issues that have such grave implications for everyone?

It Is Not Too Late

Scripture tells us not to be ignorant of our Adversary's schemes and devices.

> Lest Satan should get an advantage of us: for we are not ignorant of his devices. (2 Corinthians 2:11)

Scripture tells us that while "it is a shame" we have to talk about these things, talk about them we must. We are told to expose the hidden things of darkness by bringing them out of the darkness and into the light.

> And have no fellowship with the unfruitful works of darkness, but rather reprove *them*. For it is a shame even to speak of those things which are done of them in secret. But all things that are reproved are made manifest by the light: for whatsoever doth make manifest is light. (Ephesians 5:11-13)

And Scripture tells us to "earnestly contend for the faith."

> Beloved, when I gave all diligence to write unto you of the common salvation, it was needful for me to write unto you, and exhort you that ye should earnestly contend for the faith which was once delivered unto the saints. (Jude 3)

As I finished the writing of this book, I found out that Bruce Wilkinson had completed a "Dream Giver" television special. It was filled with Schuller terminology that further underlined the Robert Schuller concept of realizing "God's Dream." The 4-hour DVD presentation is already in Blockbuster video stores around the country and includes interviews with Rick Warren and Robert Schuller. The presentation is also being specially repackaged for specialty markets that include schools, corporations and the general public.[9]

Clearly Wilkinson is preparing the way for the proposed 2005 launch date[10] of Rick Warren's P.E.A.C.E. Plan that was already being described in explicit Schuller phraseology as "God's Dream For The World." But, in the entire 4-hour presentation, there were no words of warning from anyone about possible spiritual deception. In his interview, Robert Schuller described someone who once dared to question his theology as a "Border Bully." In the future, those who refuse to acknowledge Rick Warren's Schulleresque P.E.A.C.E. Plan as "God's Dream for the World" will probably be similarly regarded. We may all "dream" of peace, but a peace built upon the unbiblical dream theology of Robert Schuller is definitely *not* God's solution for a troubled world. Massive good works will never bring any real honor or glory to the Lord if He and His teachings are compromised in the process.

Working with the purposeful efficiency of a tightly-run Peter Drucker business corporation,[11] Rick Warren and his global alliance of Christian leaders and organizations are methodically marching the Church out of the land of biblical Christianity toward the Borderland of the New Spirituality. As he and thousands of Purpose-Driven churches around the world prepare to enact the P.E.A.C.E. Plan, there is no call in the Purpose-Driven plan to pay any heed to the Border Bereans who are scripturally challenging the wisdom of what they are doing.

It is not too late for Rick Warren to recognize that he has been greatly deceived by the worldly teachings of Robert Schuller. He could open many people's eyes if he started to expose the differences between biblical Christianity and the deceptive teachings of the New Age and its New Spirituality. He could respond to Neale Donald Walsch's "new gospel" challenge by emphatically renouncing the New Spirituality and its doctrine of "Oneness." He could make it clear to

Walsch and other New Age leaders that the spiritual "territory" of what we believe is not going to be enlarged, expanded, changed, or transcended in the name of the New Spirituality or Jabez or anyone else.

Rick Warren could make it clear that we don't need any "new revelation" because we have been given everything we need to know in properly translated Scripture and in our relationship with our Lord and Savior Jesus Christ. He could make it unmistakably clear that God is *not* "in" everyone and everything and that we will never accept the unscriptural teachings of a New Spirituality. And he could emphatically state that the true Church will not be intimidated by clever semantic labels like "exclusivistic" and "self-centered" or by the bullied threats of a "selection process."

If Rick Warren did these things he could greatly edify and encourage the body of Christ. He would be truly contending for the faith as we are admonished to do. By exposing the schemes and devices of our increasingly aggressive Adversary, he could help prevent many people from being deceived. And he could make it clear that, while we want to do whatever we can to help the world, we are not about to allow our faith or the Gospel of Jesus Christ to be compromised in the process. But it does not seem at this time that Rick Warren is about to change his course, issue the much-needed detailed warnings, and earnestly contend for the faith.

Sadly, if Rick Warren and other Christian leaders fall for New Age schemes and devices rather than exposing them, they will take countless numbers of sincere people down with them. It will be the blind leading the blind, as they fall further and further into the deceptive ditch of the New Age and its New Spirituality. Undiscerning Christians, who think they are on "the narrow way" preparing the way for Jesus Christ, may discover too late that they had actually been on "the broad way" preparing the way for Antichrist. It is not too late to warn everyone, but it must be done soon before the deception advances any further. As we have already seen, there is "another Jesus," "another Christ," "another spirit" and "another gospel" at work in the world. The Church must not continue to fall prey to the deception. And the Church must not give in to the teachings of a "New Spirituality" that promises world peace but may ultimately cost you your soul (Mark 8:36).

Ask God for Wisdom

In these times of heightened danger and treacherous deception, we must always go to the Lord for truth and direction. Christians following deceived leaders will only end up deceived themselves. We must always measure everything by the true Word of God. Seek the truth and you will find it. Knock and the door will be opened. Ask God in sincerity and in true faith, and He will give you the wisdom you need.

> If any of you lack wisdom, let him ask of God, that giveth to all men liberally, and upbraideth not; and it shall be given him. (James 1:5)

May we always have a love of the truth. May God give us wisdom and spiritual discernment as we seek to contend for the faith. And may God give us all the strength and courage and conviction to endure the challenging times that are before us.

Endnotes

Chapter 1 - The Purpose-Driven Life

1. Rick Warren, *The Purpose-Driven Life: What on Earth Am I Here For?* (Grand Rapids, Michigan: Zondervan, 2002), Dedication Page.

2. Neale Donald Walsch, *Conversations with God: an uncommon dialogue, Book 2* (Charlottesville, Virginia: Hampton Roads Publishing Company, Inc., 1997), p. 1.

3. Beliefnet Editors, *From the Ashes: A Spiritual Response to the Attack on America* (USA: Rodale Inc., 2001), p. 21.

4. Neale Donald Walsch, *Conversations with God: an uncommon dialogue, Book 1* (New York: G.P. Putnam's Sons, 1995, 1996), p. 198.

5. Neale Donald Walsch, *Conversations with God: an uncommon dialogue, Book 3* (Charlottesville, Virginia: Hampton Roads Publishing Company, Inc., 1998), p. 350.

6. Walsch, *Conversations with God: Book 1*, p. 202.

7. Neale Donald Walsch, *Tomorrow's God: Our Greatest Spiritual Challenge* (New York: Atria Books, 2004), p. 311.

8. Neale Donald Walsch, *Friendship with God: an uncommon dialogue* (New York: G.P. Putnam's Sons, 1999), p. 23.

9. Pastor Bill Randles, "An Open Letter to Neale Donald Walsch" (http://www.deceptioninthechurch.com/NealeDonaldWalsch. html).

10. Neale Donald Walsch, *The New Revelations: A Conversation with God* (New York: Atria Books, 2002), p. 157.

11. Foundation for Inner Peace, *A Course in Miracles: Combined Volume (Text, Workbook for Students, Manual for Teachers)* (Glen Ellen, California: Foundation for Inner Peace, 1975, 1992), (*Manual for Teachers*), p. 26.

12. Warren Smith, *Reinventing Jesus Christ: The New Gospel* (Ravenna, Ohio: Conscience Press, 2002), p. 34.

13. Warren Smith, *The Light that was Dark: A Spiritual Journey* (Chicago: Moody Press: Northfield Publishing, 1992), p. 144.

14. Warren, *The Purpose-Driven Life*, Dedication Page.

Chapter 2 - The Message and My 1994 Radio Warning

1. Foundation for Inner Peace, *A Course in Miracles: Combined Volume* (*Workbook*), p. 222.
2. Ibid., (*Teachers Manual*), p. 87.
3. Warren Smith, *The Light that was Dark: A Spiritual Journey*, p. 144.
4. Eugene H. Peterson, *The Message: The New Testament in Contemporary Language* (Colorado Springs, Colorado: NavPress, 1993, 2003), p. 60.

Chapter 3 - What Message?

1. Ronald S. Miller and the Editors of *New Age Journal*, *As Above, So Below: Paths to Spiritual Renewal in Daily Life* (Los Angeles: Jeremy P. Tarcher, Inc., 1992), p. xi.
2. Rick Warren, *The Purpose-Driven Life: What on Earth Am I Here For?*, p. 17, citing Eugene H. Peterson, *The Message: The New Testament in Contemporary Language*, p. 415.
3. Peterson, *The Message*, pp. 21-22.
4. Miller et al., *As Above, So Below*, p. xi.
5. Ibid.
6. Ibid., p. xiv.
7. (http://www.themystica.com/mystica/articles/a/below_above.html).
8. (http://www.mothermaryspeaks.com/as_above_so_below.htm), p. 1.
9. Helena P. Blavatsky, *The Secret Doctrine*, p. 160, quoted in "As Above, So Below" by Sri Raghavan Iyer, *Hermes*, April 1980, (http://theosophy.org/tlodocs/AsAboveSoBelow.htm), p. 1.
10. (http://www.esotericchristian.com/home.html).
11. Warren Smith, *Reinventing Jesus Christ: The New Gospel*, p. 68.
12. Ibid., p. 6.

Chapter 4 - The Kindly Christian Widow

1. Rick Warren, *The Purpose-Driven Life: What on Earth Am I Here For?*, p. 325.
2. Rick Warren, *The Purpose-Driven Church: Growth Without Compromising Your Message & Mission* (Grand Rapids, Michigan: Zondervan, 1995), p. 297.
3. Warren Smith, *The Light that was Dark: A Spiritual Journey*,

p. 141.

4. Ibid., p. 149.

Chapter 5 - Enter Robert Schuller

1. Robert H. Schuller, *Self-Esteem: The New Reformation* (Waco, Texas: Word Books, 1982), p. 19.
2. Rick Warren, *The Purpose-Driven Life: What on Earth Am I Here For?*, p. 31.
3. Warren Smith, *The Light that was Dark: A Spiritual Journey*, pp. 16-17.
4. Gerald G. Jampolsky, *Teach Only Love: The Seven Principles of Attitudinal Healing* (New York, New York: Bantam Books, 1983), pp. 11-12.
5. Ibid., p. 12.
6. Ibid., p. 13.
7. Robert Skutch, *Journey Without Distance: The Story Behind A Course in Miracles* (Berkeley, California: Celestial Arts, 1984), p. 131.
8. Ibid.
9. Gerald G. Jampolsky, *Love Is Letting Go of Fear* (Millbrae, California: Celestial Arts, 1979), p. 2.
10. Elena Oumano, *Marianne Williamson: Her Life, Her Message, Her Miracles* (New York: St. Martin's Press: St. Martin's Paperbacks, 1992), pp. 91-92.
11. Neale Donald Walsch, *Friendship with God: an uncommon dialogue*, pp. 280-283.
12. Neale Donald Walsch, *Conversations with God: an uncommon dialogue, Book 1*, pp. 1-2.
13. Bernie Siegel, *Love, Medicine & Miracles* (New York: HarperCollins Publishers: HarperPerennial, 1998), p. 18.
14. Ibid., pp. 19-20.
15. Walsch, *Friendship with God*, pp. 335-336.
16. (http://www.localcommunities.org/servlet/lc_ProcServ/dbpage=page&GID=01004011550947263615155189&PG=01004011550953336137033205).
17. Warren, *The Purpose-Driven Life*, pp. 30-31.
18. Ibid., p. 30.
19. Holy Bible, *New International Version* (Grand Rapids, Michigan: Zondervan Corporation, 1973, 1984), p. 1006.
20. Matthew Henry, *Matthew Henry's Commentary On The Whole*

Bible (Peabody, Massachusetts: Hendrickson Publishers, 1991), p. 1172.

21. Warren, *The Purpose-Driven Life*, p. 31.

22. *Hour of Power*, Robert H. Schuller, Program #1572, "Principles for Powerful, Prosperous Living—Part IX," (no specified date), (http://www.hourofpower.org/booklets/archives/pppl_1563-1573/1572.html), p. 3. Also see, Robert H. Schuller, *Believe In The God Who Believes In You* (Nashville, Tennessee: Thomas Nelson, Inc., 1989), p. 247.

23. Schuller, *Self-Esteem*, p. 19.

24. Warren, *The Purpose-Driven Life*, p. 31.

25. Ibid.

26. Robert H. Schuller, *Be Happy You Are Loved* (Nashville, Tennessee: Thomas Nelson Publishers, 1986), p. 65.

27. Schuller, *Self-Esteem*, p. 120.

28. Robert H. Schuller, *My Journey: From an Iowa Farm to a Cathedral of Dreams* (San Francisco: HarperSanFrancisco, 2001), pp. 439-440.

29. Robert H. Schuller, *Daily Power Thoughts* (New York: Jove Books, Berkeley Publishing Group, 1977, 1983), Introduction Page.

30. Robert H. Schuller, *Prayer: My Soul's Adventure With God: A Spiritual Autobiography* (Nashville, Tennessee: Thomas Nelson, Inc., 1995), Opening Page.

31. Robert H. Schuller, *Peace Of Mind Through Possibility Thinking* (Old Tappan, New Jersey: Jove Publications, Inc., 1977), pp. 137-142.

32. Robert H. Schuller, *Discover Your Possibilities* (New York: Ballantine Books, a division of Random House, 1978), pp. 128-129.

33. Dr. Paul Yonggi Cho, *The Fourth Dimension: The Key to Putting Your Faith to Work For a Successful Life* (S. Plainfield, New Jersey: Bridge Publishing, Inc., 1979), p. 44.

34. Ibid., Foreword by Robert H. Schuller.

35. Neale Donald Walsch, *The New Revelations: A Conversation with God*, p. 281.

Chapter 6 - The New Age PEACE Plan

1. Neale Donald Walsch, *The New Revelations: A Conversation with God*, p. 157.

2. Ibid., p. 282; Robert H. Schuller, *Self-Esteem: The New Reformation*, p. 38.

3. Walsch, *The New Revelations*, p. 282.
4. Ibid., p. vii.
5. Ibid., p. viii.
6. Ibid., p. 38.
7. Ibid., p. 8.
8. Ibid., p. 9.
9. Ibid., p. 175.
10. Ibid., p. 157.
11. Ibid., p. 177.
12. "The Five Steps To Peace," Conversations with God website (http://www.cwg.org/5steps/5stepstopeace.pdf), p. 1.
13. Bruce Wilkinson, *The Prayer of Jabez* (Sisters, Oregon: Multnomah Publishers, Inc., 2000), p. 13.
14. Walsch, *The New Revelations*, p. 49.
15. Ibid., p. 80.
16. Ibid., p. 279.
17. Ibid., pp. 280-281.
18. Schuller, *Self-Esteem*, pp. 38-39.
19. Walsch, *The New Revelations*, p. 282.
20. Ibid.
21. Schuller, *Self-Esteem*, p. 123.
22. March 10, 1994, Personal letter from Crystal Cathedral "Minister of Caring," Elizabeth Southard to inquiring listener.
23. April 29, 1994, Personal letter from Crystal Cathedral "Minister of Caring" to author regarding *A Course in Miracles*.
24. Schuller, *Self-Esteem*, p. 123.

Chapter 7 - What Force Drives Your Life?

1. Robert H. Schuller, *Discover Your Possibilities*, p. 3.
2. Robert H. Schuller, *If It's Going to Be, It's Up to Me: The Eight Proven Principles of Possibility Thinking* (New York: HarperPaperbacks: A Division of HarperCollins Publishers, 1997), p. 13.
3. Robert H. Schuller, *Self-Love* (New York: Jove Books, The Berkeley Publishing Group, 1969, 1978), p. 16.
4. Rick Warren, *The Purpose-Driven Life: What on Earth Am I Here For?*, p. 27.
5. Ibid.
6. Victoria Neufeldt, Editor in Chief, *Webster's New World Dictionary* (New York: Simon & Schuster, Inc., 1988), p. 416.
7. Erwin Raphael McManus, *An Unstoppable Force: Daring to*

Become the Church God Had in Mind (Loveland, Colorado: Group Publishing Inc., 2001), pp. 124-125.

8. Warren Smith, *Reinventing Jesus Christ: The New Gospel*, p. 68.

9. *Messages from Maitreya the Christ: One Hundred Forty Messages* (Los Angeles: Share International Foundation, 1980, 1992), p. 262.

10. Ibid., p. 42.

11. Ibid., p. 276.

12. Neale Donald Walsch, *The New Revelations: A Conversation with God*, p. 279.

13. Schuller, *If It's Going to Be, It's Up to Me*, p. 9.

14. Ibid., p. 222.

Chapter 8 - God is in Everything?

1. Rick Warren, *The Purpose-Driven Life: What on Earth Am I Here For?*, p. 88.

2. *Hour of Power*, Robert H. Schuller, Program #1762, "God's Word: Rebuild, Renew, Restore," November 9, 2003, (http://www.hourofpower.org/booklets/bookletdetail.cfm?ArticleID=2107), p. 5.

3. Bernie S. Siegel, *Prescriptions for Living* (New York: Harper-Perennial, A Division of HarperCollins Publishers, 1998, 1999), p. 107.

4. "Powerlines: Monthly News for Hour of Power Spiritual Share-holders and Friends," (http://www.hourofpower.org/powerlines/09.03/2004_robert_schuller_institute.cfm), p. 1.

5. *Hour of Power*, Schuller, Program #1762, p. 5.

6. Robert H. Schuller, *Self-Love*, p. 43.

7. Foundation for Inner Peace, *A Course in Miracles: Combined Volume (Workbook)*, p. 45.

8. Warren, *The Purpose-Driven Life*, p. 88, citing the *New Century Version* (Dallas, Texas: Word Publishers, 1991).

9. Barbara Stahura, "Allowing Success: An Interview with Dr. Wayne Dyer," *Science of Mind*, September 2004, Vol. 77, No. 9, p. 87.

10. Eugene H. Peterson, *The Message: The New Testament in Contemporary Language*, p. 400.

11. Foundation for Inner Peace, *A Course in Miracles: Combined Volume (Workbook)*, p. 45.

12. Ibid., (*Text*), p. 125.

13. *Messages from Maitreya the Christ: One Hundred Forty Messages,* p. 88.
14. Ibid., p. 23.
15. Ibid., p. 203.
16. Siegel, *Prescriptions for Living,* p. 107.
17. Bernie S. Siegel, *How To Live Between Office Visits* (New York: HarperCollins Publishers, Inc., 1993), p. 180.
18. Neale Donald Walsch, *Friendship with God: an uncommon dialogue,* pp. 295-296.

Chapter 9 - Robert Schuller and Jerry Jampolsky

1. Robert H. Schuller, *Robert Schuller Presents His Legacy of Hope: The Be Happy Attitudes: Eight Positive Attitudes that can Transform Your Life* (Dallas, Texas: Word Publishing, 1996), Videocassette #2 (Session 6).
2. *Hour of Power,* Robert H. Schuller, "Become a Peace Maker," 2003, (http://www.hourofpower.org/helpforyou/personal_detail. cfm?ArticleID=1867), p. 2.
3. Gerald G. Jampolsky, *Love Is Letting Go of Fear,* Dedication Page.
4. *Reinventing Jesus Christ: The New Gospel* can be downloaded free from the Internet (http://www.reinventingjesuschrist.com).
5. Foundation for Inner Peace, *A Course in Miracles: Combined Volume* (Text), p. 52.
6. Ibid.
7. Ibid., p. 147.
8. Ibid., p. 100.
9. Ibid. (*Workbook*), p. 183.
10. Ibid. (*Text*), p. 237.
11. Ibid. (*Manual*), p. 88.
12. Robert H. Schuller, *Self-Esteem: The New Reformation,* p. 51.
13. Foundation for Inner Peace, *A Course in Miracles, Combined Volume* (*Workbook*), p. 413.
14. Robert H. Schuller, *The Be (Happy) Attitudes: Eight Positive Attitudes that Can Transform Your Life!* (New York: Bantam Books, 1985, 1987), p. 150.
15. Personal notes from Johanna Michaelsen's telephone call to the Crystal Cathedral on October 3, 1985. Used with permission.
16. Telephone conversation with Conrad Hanson at the Miracle Distribution Center on November 5, 2003.
17. Schuller, *Robert Schuller Presents His Legacy of Hope,* Videocas-

sette #2 (Session 6).

18. *Hour of Power*, Robert H. Schuller, Program #1782, "Live Life at Its Best—Part IX," March 28, 2004, (http://www.hourofpower. org/booklets/bookletdetail.cfm?ArticleID=2350), pp. 4-5.

19. (http://www.hourofpower.org/interviews/interviews_detail.cfm? ArticleID=3079).

20. The Miracle Distribution Center website (http://www.miracle center.org/ssl/catpt04a.htm), Section 4a, p. 1.

21. (http://www.hourofpower.org) and (http://www.store.yahoo.com/cathedral-gifts/fobo.html).

22. *Hour of Power*, October 17, 2004, Robert H. Schuller's interview of Jerry Jampolsky. (This comment made by Schuller was in the televised interview but did not make it into their written transcript.)

23. Personal letter of April 29, 1994, from the Crystal Cathedral "Minister of Caring." See Chapter 6.

24. Rick Warren, *The Purpose-Driven Church: Growth Without Compromising Your Message & Mission*, p. 190.

Chapter 10 - Robert Schuller and Rick Warren

1. *Hour of Power*, Robert H. Schuller, Program #1783, "What Will Be The Future of This Ministry?," April 4, 2004, (http://www. hourofpower.org/booklets/bookletdetail.cfm?ArticleID=2570), p. 4.

2. Tim Stafford, "A Regular Purpose-Driven Guy," *Christianity Today*, November 18, 2002, Vol. 46, No. 12, (http://www. christianitytoday.com/ct/2002/012/l.42.html), p. 4.

3. Ibid., p. 5.

4. Rick Warren, *The Purpose-Driven Church: Growth Without Compromising Your Message & Mission*, p. 43.

5. Ibid.

6. Ibid., p. 398.

7. Robert H. Schuller, *Your Church Has A Fantastic Future!: A Possibility Thinker's Guide To A Successful Church* (Ventura, California: Regal Books, 1986), p. 235.

8. Robert H. Schuller, *Move Ahead with Possibility Thinking* (Old Tappan, New Jersey: Fleming H. Revell Company: Spire Books, 1967, 1974), p. 19.

9. Robert H. Schuller, *Life's Not Fair, But God Is Good* (New York: Bantam Books, 1991, 1993), pp. 54-55.

10. Rick Warren, *The Purpose-Driven Life: What on Earth Am I Here For?*, p. 285.
11. Robert H. Schuller, *Self-Love*, p. 23.
12. The Theosophical Society In England: (http://www.theosophical-society.org.uk/html/ttsie_objectives.html), pp. 1-2.
13. Warren, *The Purpose-Driven Life*, p. 33.
14. Ibid., p. 248.
15. Marilyn Ferguson, *The Aquarian Conspiracy: Personal and Social Transformation In the 1980's* (Los Angeles: J.P. Tarcher, Inc. 1980), p. 375.
16. Ibid.
17. Warren, *The Purpose-Driven Life*, p. 113.
18. Ibid., p. 157.
19. Ibid., p. 213.
20. Robert H. Schuller, *Success Is Never Ending, Failure Is Never Final* (New York: Bantam Books, 1988, 1990), p. 151.
21. Robert H. Schuller, *If It's Going to Be, It's Up to Me*, p. 218.
22. Robert H. Schuller, *My Journey: From an Iowa Farm to a Cathedral of Dreams*, p. 474.
23. Schuller, *If It's Going to Be, It's Up to Me*, p. 142.
24. Ibid., p. 144.
25. Ibid., p. 146.
26. Ibid.
27. Warren, *The Purpose-Driven Life*, p. 238.
28. Ibid.
29. Ibid., p. 239.
30. Schuller, *If It's Going to Be, It's Up to Me*, p. 139.
31. Warren, *The Purpose-Driven Life*, p. 203.
32. Schuller, *If It's Going to Be, It's Up to Me*, p. 97.
33. Warren, *The Purpose-Driven Life*, p. 300.
34. Ibid., p. 301.
35. Schuller, *Move Ahead with Possibility Thinking*, p. 190.
36. Ibid., p. 188.
37. Warren, *The Purpose-Driven Life*, p. 301.
38. Robert H. Schuller, *You Can Become The Person You Want To Be* (Old Tappan, New Jersey: Spire Books published by Jove Publications, 1973, 1978), p. 25.
39. Robert H. Schuller, *Prayer: My Soul's Adventure With God*, p. 90.
40. Warren, *The Purpose-Driven Church*, p. 20.

Chapter 11 - God's Dream?

1. Robert H. Schuller, *Reach Out for New Life* (New York: Hawthorn Books, Inc., 1977), p. 51.
2. Robert H. Schuller, *Self-Esteem: The New Reformation*, p. 102.
3. Bruce Wilkinson, *The Dream Giver* (Sisters, Oregon: Multnomah Publishers, 2003), p. 15.
4. Ibid., p. 6.
5. Schuller, *Move Ahead with Possibility Thinking*, p. 188.
6. Ibid., p. 15.
7. Ibid., p. 21.
8. Ibid., p. 23.
9. Ibid., p. 48.
10. Ibid., pp. 53-54.
11. Ibid., p. 65.
12. Ibid., p. 69.
13. Ibid., p. 72.
14. Ibid., pp. 77-78.
15. Ibid., p. 111.
16. Ibid.
17. Ibid., p. 121.
18. Ibid., p. 136.
19. *Hour of Power*, Bruce Wilkinson, Program #1760, "Living the Dream," October 26, 2003, (http://www.hourofpower.org/booklets/bookletdetail.cfm?ArticleID=2087), p. 1.
20. Ibid.
21. Ibid.
22. Ibid., p. 8.
23. Ibid.
24. Ibid., p. 9.
25. Saddleback Church, October 26, 2003. Internet broadcast from Saddleback Church, transcribed by author.
26. Schuller, *Self-Esteem*, p. 119.
27. Ibid., p. 104.
28. Ibid., p. 105.
29. Ibid., p. 75.
30. Ibid.
31. Ibid., p. 118.
32. Ibid., p. 112.
33. National Association of Evangelicals: Annual conference, March 11, 2004, Robert Schuller, NAE Compact Disc.

34. Wayne Dyer, *You'll See It When You Believe It: The Way to Your Personal Transformation* (New York: Avon Books, 1989), p. 96.
35. Ibid., p. 97.
36. Ibid., p. 98.
37. Robert H. Schuller, *My Journey: From an Iowa Farm to a Cathedral of Dreams*, p. 492.
38. Ibid., p. 502.
39. Neale Donald Walsch, *The New Revelations: A Conversation with God*, pp. 7-8.

Chapter 12 - Rick Warren's P.E.A.C.E. Plan

1. Robert H. Schuller, *If It's Going to Be, It's Up to Me*, p. 193.
2. Rick Warren, Saddleback Church e-mail, October 27, 2003, "GOD'S DREAM FOR YOU—AND THE WORLD!"
3. Rick Warren, Saddleback Church Sermon, November 2, 2003, "Our Global P.E.A.C.E. Plan," transcribed from Internet broadcast by author.
4. Weekend Message Application Guide: "Our Global P.E.A.C.E. Plan," November 1-2, 2003, (http://www.saddleback.com/maturity/fullstory.asp?type=238), p. 2.
5. Neale Donald Walsch, *Tomorrow's God: Our Greatest Spiritual Challenge*, p. ix.
6. Warren, Saddleback Church e-mail, October 27, 2003.
7. Robert H. Schuller, *Discover Your Possibilities*, p. 100.
8. Warren, Saddleback Church e-mail, October 27, 2003.
9. The Oprah Winfrey Show, Marianne Williamson as guest, "What Really Matters Now," September 26, 2001 transcript (Livingston, New Jersey: Burrelle's Information Services), pp. 10, 13.
10. Wayne Dyer, "There's a Spiritual Solution to Every Problem," PBS Broadcast, 2001, transcribed by author.
11. Ibid.
12. Rick Warren, *The Purpose-Driven Church: Growth Without Compromising Your Message & Mission*, p. 190.
13. *Hour of Power*, Robert H. Schuller, Program #1783, "What Will Be The Future of This Ministry?," April 4, 2004, (http://www.hourofpower.org/booklets/bookletdetail.cfm?ArticleID=2570), p. 4.

Chapter 13 - Deceived about Deception

1. Robert H. Schuller, *Discover Your Possibilities*, p. 61.

2. Rick Warren, *The Purpose-Driven Life: What on Earth Am I Here For?*, p. 203.
3. Ibid., p. 285.
4. Ibid.
5. Ibid., pp. 285-286.
6. Wayne Dyer, "The Power of Intention," PBS Broadcast, 2004, transcribed by author.
7. (http://www.powerofpurpose.org/judges_warren.html) or (http://www.pastors.com/article.asp?artid=5657).
8. "Biography: Sir John Templeton," John Templeton Foundation website (http://www.templeton.org/sir_John_Templeton/index.asp), p. 2.
9. (http://www.geocities.com/endtimedeception/berean.htm), p. 5.
10. Kathy Juline, "Question Authority: A Conversation with Neale Donald Walsch," *Science of Mind*, May 2004, p. 29.

Chapter 14 - False Christ with a Purpose

1. *Messages from Maitreya the Christ: One Hundred Forty Messages*, p. 123.
2. Ibid., p. 23.
3. Ibid., p. 123.
4. Ibid., p. 88.
5. Ibid., p. 203.
6. Ibid., p. 183.
7. Ibid., p. 218.
8. Ibid., p. 45.
9. Ibid., p. 44.
10. Ibid., p. 150.
11. Wayne S. Peterson, *Extraordinary Times, Extraordinary Beings: Experiences of an American Diplomat with Maitreya and the Masters of Wisdom* (Henderson, Nevada: Emergence Press, 2001), p. 38.
12. Ibid., p. 35.
13. Ibid., p. 100.
14. Wayne S. Peterson, author, interviewed on *Bridging Heaven & Earth*, a weekly talk show broadcast on Cox Communications' public access channel 17 in Santa Barbara, California on November 9, 2001, Videocassette, (http://www.HeaventoEarth.com).
15. *Messages from Maitreya the Christ*, p. 6.
16. Ibid., p. 248.

17. Benjamin Creme, *The Reappearance of the Christ and the Masters of Wisdom* (London, England: The Tara Press, 1980), p. 30.
18. *Messages from Maitreya the Christ*, p. 206.
19. Ibid., p. 266.
20. Ibid., p. 159.
21. Ibid., p. 183.
22. Ibid., p. 192.
23. Ibid., p. 153.
24. Ibid., p. 56.
25. Ibid., p. 123.
26. Creme, *The Reappearance of the Christ and the Masters of Wisdom*, p. 39.
27. Alice Bailey and Djwhal Khul, *The Reappearance of the Christ*, Chapter 6 - The New World Religion, (Caux, Switzerland: Netnews Association and/or its suppliers, 2002), (http://www. netnews. org).
28. Tom Holladay and Kay Warren, *Foundations Participant's Guide: 11 Core Truths To Build Your Life On* (Grand Rapids, Michigan: Zondervan, 2003), p. 46.
29. *Hour of Power*, Robert H. Schuller, Program #1762, "God's Word: Rebuild, Renew, Restore," November 9, 2003, (http:// www.hourofpower.org/booklets/bookletdetail.cfm?ArticleID = 2107), p. 5.
30. Ronald S. Miller and the Editors of *New Age Journal, As Above, So Below*, p. xi.
31. Rick Warren, *The Purpose-Driven Life: What on Earth Am I Here For?*, p. 172.
32. Creme, *The Reappearance of the Christ and the Masters of Wisdom*, p. 46.
33. Ibid., p. 85.
34. Ibid., p. 46.
35. Eugene H. Peterson, *The Message: The New Testament in Contemporary Language*, p. 535.
36. *Messages from Maitreya the Christ*, p. 248.
37. Ibid., p. 189.
38. Barbara Marx Hubbard, *The Revelation: A Message of Hope for the New Millennium* (Novato, California: Nataraj Publishing, 1995), p. 233.
39. Ibid., p. 255.
40. Ibid., p. 240.

41. Warren Smith, *Reinventing Jesus Christ: The New Gospel*, pp. 60-61.

42. Ibid., p. 67.

Chapter 15 - Contend for the Faith

1. Robert H. Schuller, *Self-Esteem: The New Reformation*, pp. 25, 38.

2. Rick Warren, Saddleback Sermon, November 2, 2003, "Our Global P.E.A.C.E. Plan," transcribed from Internet broadcast by author.

3. Schuller, *Self-Esteem*, pp. 75, 104-105.

4. Rick Warren, Saddleback Church e-mail, October 27, 2003, "GOD'S DREAM FOR YOU—AND THE WORLD!"

5. Robert H. Schuller, *Self-Love*, p. 43.

6. Rick Warren, *The Purpose-Driven Life: What on Earth Am I Here For?*, p. 88.

7. Matthew Henry, *Matthew Henry's Commentary On The Whole Bible*, p. 1646.

8. Warren Smith, *Reinventing Jesus Christ: The New Gospel*, pp. 66-67.

9. Bruce Wilkinson, *The Dream Giver*, DVD (New York: GoodTimes Entertainment, 2004).

10. (http://www.floridabaptistwitness.com/2523.article), Vol. 121, No. 20, May 6, 2004.

11. Lynn D. Leslie, Sarah H. Leslie and Susan J. Conway, *The Pied Pipers of Purpose: Part I: Human Capital Systems and Church Performance* (Ravenna, Ohio: Conscience Press, 2004), (http://discernment-ministries.com), pp. 23-24.

Bibliography

Beliefnet Editors. *From the Ashes: A Spiritual Response to the Attack on America*. USA: Rodale Inc., 2001.

Cho, Dr. Paul Yonggi. *The Fourth Dimension: The Key to Putting Your Faith to Work For a Successful Life*. S. Plainfield, New Jersey: Bridge Publishing, Inc., 1979.

Creme, Benjamin. *The Reappearance of the Christ and the Masters of Wisdom*. London, England: The Tara Press, 1980.

Dyer, Wayne. *You'll See It When You Believe It: The Way to Your Personal Transformation*. New York, New York: Avon Books, 1989.

Ferguson, Marilyn. *The Aquarian Conspiracy: Personal and Social Transformation In the 1980's*. New York: J.P. Tarcher, Inc., 1980.

Foundation for Inner Peace. *A Course in Miracles, Combined Volume (Text, Workbook for Students, Manual for Teachers)*. Glen Ellen, California: Foundation for Inner Peace, 1975, 1992.

Henry, Matthew. *Matthew Henry's Commentary On The Whole Bible*. Peabody, Massachusetts: Hendrickson Publishers, 1991.

Holladay, Tom and Warren, Kay. *Foundations Participant's Guide: 11 Core Truths To Build Your Life On*. Grand Rapids, Michigan: Zondervan, 2003.

Holy Bible. *New International Version*. Grand Rapids, Michigan: Zondervan Corporation, 1973, 1984.

Hubbard, Barbara Marx. *The Revelation: A Message of Hope for the New Millennium*. Novato, California: Nataraj Publishing, 1993, 1995.

Jampolsky, Gerald G. *Love Is Letting Go of Fear*. Millbrae, California: Celestial Arts, 1979.

Jampolsky, Gerald G. *Teach Only Love: The Seven Principles of Attitudinal Healing*. New York, New York: Bantam Books, 1983.

Leslie, Lynn D., Leslie, Sarah H. and Conway, Susan J. *The Pied Pipers of Purpose: Part 1: Human Capital Systems and Church Performance*. Ravenna, Ohio: Conscience Press, 2004.

McManus, Erwin Raphael. *An Unstoppable Force: Daring to Become the Church God had in Mind.* Loveland, Colorado: Group Publishing, 2001.

Messages from Maitreya the Christ: One Hundred Forty Messages. Los Angeles: Share International Foundation, 1980, 2001.

Miller, Ronald S. and The Editors of *New Age Journal. As Above, So Below.* Los Angeles: Jeremy P. Tarcher, Inc., 1992.

Neufeldt, Victoria, Editor in Chief. *Webster's New World Dictionary.* New York: Simon & Schuster, Inc., 1988.

Oumano, Elena. *Marianne Williamson: Her Life, Her Message, Her Miracles.* New York: St. Martin's Paperbacks, 1992.

Peterson, Eugene H. *The Message: The New Testament in Contemporary Language.* Colorado Springs, Colorado: NavPress, 1993, 2003.

Peterson, Wayne S. *Extraordinary Times, Extraordinary Beings: Experiences of an American Diplomat with Maitreya and the Masters of Wisdom.* Henderson, Nevada: Emergence Press, 2001.

Schuller, Robert H. *Be Happy You Are Loved.* Nashville, Tennessee: Thomas Nelson Publishers, 1986.

Schuller, Robert H. *Believe In The God Who Believes In You.* Nashville, Tennessee: Thomas Nelson, Inc., 1989.

Schuller, Robert H. *Daily Power Thoughts.* New York: Jove Books, The Berkley Publishing Group, 1977, 1983.

Schuller, Robert H. *Discover Your Possibilities.* New York: Ballantine Books, 1978, 1990.

Schuller, Robert H. *If It's Going to Be, It's Up to Me: The Eight Proven Principles of Possibility Thinking.* New York: HarperPaperbacks, 1997, 1998.

Schuller, Robert H. *Life's Not Fair, but God is Good.* New York: Bantam Books, 1991, 1993.

Schuller, Robert H. *Move Ahead with Possibility Thinking.* Old Tappan, New Jersey: Spire Books, Fleming H. Revell Company, 1967, 1974.

Schuller, Robert H. *My Journey: From an Iowa Farm to a Cathedral of Dreams.* San Francisco: HarperSanFrancisco, 2001.

Schuller, Robert H. *Peace Of Mind Through Possibility Thinking*. Old Tappan, New Jersey: Jove Publications, Inc., 1977.

Schuller, Robert H. *Prayer: My Soul's Adventure With God: A Spiritual Autobiography*. Nashville, Tennessee: Thomas Nelson, Inc., 1995.

Schuller, Robert H. *Reach Out for New Life*. New York: Hawthorn Books, Inc., 1977.

Schuller, Robert H. *Robert Schuller Presents His Legacy of Hope: The Be Happy Attitudes: Eight Positive Attitudes that can Transform Your Life*. (video, cassette, book set). Dallas, Texas: Word Publishing, 1996.

Schuller, Robert H. *Self-Esteem: The New Reformation*. Waco, Texas: Word Books, 1982.

Schuller, Robert H. *Self-Love*. New York: Jove Books, The Berkley Publishing Group, 1969, 1978.

Schuller, Robert H. *Success Is Never Ending, Failure Is Never Final*. New York: Bantam Books, 1988, 1990.

Schuller, Robert H. *The Be (Happy) Attitudes: 8 Positive Attitudes That Can Transform Your Life!*. New York: Bantam Books, 1985, 1987.

Schuller, Robert H. *You Can Become The Person You Want to Be*. Old Tappan, New Jersey: Spire Books, Jove Publications, 1973, 1978.

Schuller, Robert H. *Your Church Has A Fantastic Future!: A Possibility Thinker's Guide To A Successful Church*. Ventura, California: Regal Books, 1986.

Siegel, Bernie S. *How to Live Between Office Visits*. New York: Harper-Collins Publishers, 1993.

Siegel, Bernie S. *Love, Medicine & Miracles*. New York: Harper-Perennial, 1986, 1998.

Siegel, Bernie S. *Peace, Love & Healing: Bodymind Communication & The Path To Self-Healing: An Exploration*. New York: Harper-Perrenial, 1989.

Siegel, Bernie S. *Prescriptions for Living*. New York: HarperPerennial, 1998, 1999.

Skutch, Robert. *Journey Without Distance: The Story Behind A Course in Miracles*. Berkeley, California: Celestial Arts, 1984.

Smith, Warren. *Reinventing Jesus Christ: The New Gospel*. Ravenna, Ohio: Conscience Press, 2002.

Smith, Warren. *The Light that was Dark: A Spiritual Journey*. Chicago: Moody Press: Northfield Publishing, 1992.

Walsch, Neale Donald. *Conversations with God: an uncommon dialogue, Book 1*. New York: G.P. Putnam's Sons, 1995, 1996.

Walsch, Neale Donald. *Conversations with God: an uncommon dialogue, Book 2*. Charlottesville, Virginia: Hampton Roads Publishing Company, Inc., 1997.

Walsch, Neale Donald. *Conversations with God: an uncommon dialogue, Book 3*. Charlottesville, Virginia: Hampton Roads Publishing Company, Inc., 1998.

Walsch, Neale Donald. *Friendship with God: an uncommon dialogue*. New York: G.P. Putnam's Sons, 1999.

Walsch, Neale Donald. *The New Revelations: A Conversation with God*. New York: Atria Books, 2002.

Walsch, Neale Donald. *Tomorrow's God: Our Greatest Spiritual Challenge*. New York: Atria Books, 2004.

Warren, Rick. *The Purpose-Driven Church: Growth Without Compromising Your Message & Mission*. Grand Rapids, Michigan: Zondervan, 1995.

Warren, Rick. *The Purpose-Driven Life: What on Earth Am I Here For?*. Grand Rapids, Michigan: Zondervan, 2002.

Wilkinson, Bruce. *The Dream Giver*. Sisters, Oregon: Multnomah Publishers, Inc., 2003.

Wilkinson, Bruce. *The Prayer of Jabez*. Sisters, Oregon: Multnomah Publishers, Inc., 2000.

Index

D